Radical Economics

General Editor: SAM AARONOVITCH

Debates between economists are not just technical arguments amongst practitioners but often reflect philosophical and ideological positions which are not always made explicit.

Discontent grew with the prevailing economic orthodoxy as the long period of economic expansion in the advanced capitalist economies came to an end in the 1970s; disenchantment was expressed in open discussion about the 'crisis' in economics and in the rise of various kinds of radical economic theory, often using the general title of 'political economy'.

Many economists have looked for a more fruitful point of departure in the ideas of Marx and the classical economists and also in such contemporary economists as Kalecki and Sraffa. Although it is possible to identify a broad radical stream, it does not mean that there are no significant controversies within this radical approach and, indeed, it would be unhealthy if this were not the case.

Can radical economic theory interpret the world better than the current orthodoxy which it challenges? And can it show also how to change it? This is a challenge which this series proposes to take up, adding to work already being done.

Each book will be a useful contribution to its particular field and should become a text around which the study of economics takes place.

Radical Economics

Published

Keith Cowling, *Monopoly Capitalism*
Michael Howard, *Profits in Economic Theory*

Forthcoming

Amit Bhaduri, *Macroeconomics*
Michael Bleaney, *The Rise and Fall of Keynesian Economics*
Terry Byres, *The Political Economy of Poor Nations*
Matthew Edel, *Urban Economics*
David Purdy, *The Theory of Wages*

Profits in Economic Theory

MICHAEL HOWARD

Associate Professor of Economics,
University of Waterloo, Ontario, Canada

First published 1983 by
THE MACMILLAN PRESS LTD
London and Basingstoke
Companies and representatives throughout the world

ISBN 0 333 32165 0 (hard cover)
ISBN 0 333 32166 9 (paper cover)

Typeset in Great Britain by
STYLESET LIMITED
Salisbury, Wiltshire

Printed in Hong Kong

Contents

Acknowledgements

Work on the topics discussed in this book began several years ago and I am greatly indebted to many people who offered suggestions and criticisms. In this regard I would like to thank Sam Aaronovitch, John Bonner, Ian Bradley, Peter Jackson, John King, Ronald Meek, Fadle Naqib, Lionel Needleman and John Winckler. Thanks are also due to Keith Povey for editorial services and to Debbie Pallas and Ann Wendt for secretarial assistance.

University of Waterloo   Michael Howard
Ontario, Canada
October 1982

Part I
INTRODUCTION

1
Profit in Economic Theory

The connection between profit and economic theory is an intimate one. Economic analysis, in very large part, developed only with the maturing of a capitalist system in which production activities became overwhelmingly organised on the basis of profitability. Moreover, the attempt to understand such a system has been the focal point of economic interest ever since. However, a generally accepted theory of profit has not emerged at any stage in the history of economics. The current state of affairs is no exception to this. Various concepts of profit and of the 'profit system' abound, different strands of analysis show few signs of convergence and theoretical controversies remain intense.

The reasons for this are undoubtedly due in part to the intellectual difficulties inherent in the analysis of social phenomena. But there are also deeper reasons. As individuals, social scientists come to their profession rather late in life, so that pre-analytic visions of their subject, together with the emotional energy these incorporate, are already well formed. In addition, powerful interests are also involved. The conclusions of economic theory are viewed as socially neutral only by the naive. They are easily subsumed in fact, into evaluations of the institutions of capitalist economies.

This book deals with the principal theories of profit which have emerged since the early nineteenth century when formal economic analysis began to flower. This means that there is a huge mass of available literature to consider, so some devices have had to be employed in order to reduce it to manageable proportions. One of the simplest, although more controversial, has been to disregard some analysis altogether. The most significant omission is that work which deals with international economic relations. Throughout the following chapters, a closed economy is assumed. The primary victim here is that Marxist literature which considers imperialism to be essential to the understanding of profits. Other topics which receive scant treatment are issues connected with monopoly power. This is mainly because of the great conceptual difficulties faced in seriously presenting this subject within the very restricted space that can be allotted to it. In addition, some important economists are ignored. The most eminent is undoubtedly Marshall. However, this omission is less serious than appearances suggest. Marshall's discussion of profit was not idiosyncratic and its substance is incorporated in the discussion of other neoclassical economists. The convention has also been adopted of dealing with the most modern version of any particular theory. The only grounds for departing from this practice is when other theories have a special significance in their own right, or when the historical development of the theory throws special light upon more recent formulations.

Finally, since there still remains a great deal of diverse theory pertaining to profits, some principles of organisation through which *general* types of approach may be located prove useful. Here the standards of selection by which economists are grouped result in separating out three broad orientations to the understanding of profit. They are the surplus approach, supply and demand analysis and the principle of effective demand. There are many reasons recommending these divisions, but not least in importance is that they underlie much contemporary controversy in economic theory.

There are drawbacks, however. Any organisation such as this is an imposed one and the various approaches take on definite contours not always so clearly inherent in the work of the individual economists. Consequently, the interpretation of some economists' work has often been rather brutal. Qualifications which they made and ambiguities which they failed to overcome are played down. Furthermore, any analysis of the historical influences gained by particular ideas is greatly circumscribed. In other words, organisation is always to some extent a libel upon intellectual history, but unless one reprints authors verbatim there is really no other way to proceed.

Each of the approaches discussed in Parts II, III and V provides a different theoretical orientation towards the understanding of profit. The general principles are outlined in Chapters 2, 9 and 16. However, despite these differences, each focuses upon the same substantive issues and employs similar procedures in the analysis. The three main problems dealt with are the determinants of profits and the rate of profit, the relationship between profits and other economic phenomena and, to lesser extent, the course of profits in capitalist development.

In dealing with these problems all three approaches employ the same general methodology. At the formal level at least, all three focus upon the determinants of *equilibrium* profits and upon the relationship of profits to other phenomena within *equilibria*. Although the precise conception of what constitutes an equilibrium does vary, in all cases it is conceived as a terminal state, a situation in which certain specified economic forces have completely worked themselves out. The differences between the three types of analysis on this matter are limited to which economic forces are the important ones to consider and how, in fact, particular economic forces work themselves out.

Furthermore, the concept of determination is essentially the same. In all cases the analysis proceeds in terms of models whose elements are dichotomised into *exogenous* and *endogenous* components, and the terms *determination* or *causation* refer to the relationship between these two types of component. The exogenous elements are those which are taken as given in the analysis. They encompass the values of particular magnitudes and the relationships between certain variables. There is no implication that these components are not themselves determined, only that their determinants lie outside the range of the model in which they are considered to be exogenous. The endogenous components, on the other hand, are those which are to be determined within the model. They are determined in the sense that the exogenous components constrain the set of values which they may take. Thus it can be said that the exogenous components determine, or cause, these values taken by the endogenous components.

This distinction may be illustrated by considering a procedure typically adopted in the surplus approach which is the subject-matter of Part II. In this type of economics, technological relationships between inputs and outputs together with the prevailing wage rate are frequently taken as given, or predetermined, in the analysis of the profit rate and commodity prices. Consequently, technology and the magnitude of the wage are considered to be exogenous, while the rate of profit and prices are considered to be endogenous variables. These endogenous variables will take different values depending upon what is assumed about the exogenous components: for example, at what level the wage rate is assumed to be fixed. In this sense the exogenous components determine the values of the endogenous variables.

The classification of elements into exogenous and endogenous relates to their role in a specific model. A particular magnitude may be considered exogenous in one model and endogenous in another. Indeed, one of the main differences between the various approaches discussed in the following chapters concerns what they class as 'exogenous' and 'endogenous' in the investigation of profits. Surplus theorists adopt one set of conventions, supply and demand theorists adopt an alternative one and theorists of effective demand yet another. These different procedures reflect different views of how a capitalist system actually operates.

Yet another common thread in the work examined here is its theoretical nature. Each approach highlights particular phenomena relative to others and totally abstracts from a great many others. The purpose, in each case, is to concentrate upon that which is thought to be essential and not to be descriptively 'realistic'. This means that the focus is upon 'pure' forms, unencumbered with the complexities inherent in 'real' economies. Thus, for example, many theorists frequently assume a closed economy with homogeneous labour and free land. It is not implied that international economic relations, heterogeneous labour and scarce natural resources are totally without relevance to the analysis of profits. Abstraction from these phenomena only reflects the presumption that they are of secondary significance and can be disregarded, therefore, at least in the early stages of theory-building. Consequently, although the economic models with which theorists work may never be observed in their pure form, even approximately, the conclusions yielded are nevertheless thought to be necessary for understanding actual economies, since they incorporate the fundamental relationships of these economies. Thus to criticise abstract theory on the grounds of 'unrealism' *per se* is to miss the point of the exercise.

Theory construction in all types of economics has become increasingly formal. In modern economic theory assumptions tend to be clearly specified, conclusions precisely stated and the deduction rigorous. One manifestation of this is the increasing use of mathematics in theory construction. The text of the following chapters does not fully incorporate this aspect into the discussion. In particular very little mathematical reasoning is employed and the mathematical notation has been reduced to an absolute minimum. This may have engendered a clumsy treatment of some issues, together with a false impression of the texture of modern economics. I hope that more serious defects have not materialised. In any event ample references are provided where a more formal and typical treatment is provided.

Finally, there is the question of radical political economy or radical economics to consider. The prevailing view on this matter among economists is that all three approaches considered here can serve radical purposes. It is held that there are important elements in each type of analysis which can be utilised to develop a thoroughgoing critique of capitalist economic systems. It is further maintained that every approach can provide guides to action for those seeking fundamental change of such systems. Thus from this perspective there is no radical economic theory as distinct from conventional economics, there is only a difference in how economics is utilised.

However, supply and demand theory has almost invariably generated a hostile reaction from radicals themselves. They have tended to view it as a thinly veiled device for representing capitalist economies in a more favourable light than reality warrants in order to legitimise the position of economically dominant classes. It is also charged that its particular manner of conceptualising economic phenomena is inherently biased to this task and that any potentially radical implications which do emerge are anaesthetised or represented as justifying only system-preserving reforms.

Coupled with this has generally been some ambivalence towards theories of effective demand, especially toward the most developed Keynesian version of these theories. Certainly, few, if any, radicals would want to quarrel with the central proposition of this theory, namely that capitalist economies can experience situations involving large-scale unemployment in which countervailing forces are weak or non-existent. It is also true that some economists have built a radicalism centred upon the effective demand crises associated with capitalism. Others, however, have been uneasy with the structure of Keynesian economics. The chief problem here is that Keynesian concepts show similar characteristics to those of supply and demand theory. Rather naturally, then, hostility to the latter has flowed over to Keynesian analysis as well, and the surplus approach alone, or particular variants within it, has been regarded as radical economic theory *par excellence*, i.e. as the most appropriate framework from which to counter orthodoxy and rally opposition.

Nevertheless even from this latter perspective there still remains a rationale for radicals seriously to study economics other than that of the surplus approach. In addition to the obvious point that an ideology has to be understood before it can be cogently undermined, there is a more positive purpose to which such study can be put. As we shall see in Part IV, modern formulations of supply and demand theory highlight important analytical limitations in all variants of the surplus approach. Consequently the further development of radical economics itself can potentially benefit from a serious consideration of alternative theoretical systems.

Part II
PROFIT IN SURPLUS THEORY

2
Characteristics of Surplus Theory

Surplus Defined

The principal characteristic of this approach to economic theory is the concentration of analysis upon the surplus as it arises in different types of economic system. The notion of what comprises surplus differs between theorists but the essential idea remains the same. Surplus constitutes *disposable* resources. The output of any economic system is divided into two components. There is that which is required for the reproduction of the output, and thereby represents necessary costs of production or necessary costs of reproduction. The remaining component can then be regarded as *disposable*. The system's output can be ensured irrespective of its utilisation. The economic theory which we are about to consider seeks to explain the nature of the surplus, its origin and determinants, its measurement and valuation, and its utilisation in different activities.

The main focus of attention has been on these problems as they pertain to capitalist economies. These are defined by the specific form of the relations which exist between economic agents. They encompass those economies involving private ownership of the means of production and the institution of wage labour. In any system where private ownership concentrates control of the means of production into the hands of a sub-set of economic agents, the remaining agents cannot 'work for themselves' but must interact with the owners in order to gain access to these means of production. There are many forms which this interaction can take. In capitalism it is based upon the principle of 'free' or 'market' exchange of labour services for wages.[1] The owners of the means of production utilise these labour services in production activities and normally receive revenues over and above the costs involved. Such revenues constitute profits and rents. Profits are the revenues derived from the ownership of capital goods, i.e. produced means of production, and rents are those arising from the ownership of natural resources.

As we shall see in subsequent chapters, theorists of the surplus approach in economic theory have generally regarded profits as constituting the major component of the surplus in a capitalist economy. The theory of profit is therefore at the very centre of this type of economics. Consequently, analysis has concentrated on the origin, determinants, measurement and valuation of profits. In addition, the allocation of profits between capital accumulation and consumption, and the effect which different utilisations have for the operation of the system, have been investigated.

Methods of Analysing the Surplus

Economists who have taken the concept of the surplus as an organising principle of their work have evolved various methods of analysis. Many of these are common methods, in that later theorists have borrowed and built upon the work of their predecessors. This is especially true of the leading lights of this approach. Ricardo (1817) erected his economics on the basis of a critical examination of Smith (1776). Marx (1867) subsequently took Ricardo as a principal guide, and Sraffa (1960) in turn acknowledged that his primary intellectual debts were to these classics. Consequently, there are great similarities in the methods employed. In this section we consider these methods.

We have already indicated in the preceeding section that one common element has been the attention given to the capitalist form of economy. This is defined in class terms. Naturally, therefore, economic agents are categorised into classes. Sometimes in economic analysis such a typology of agents represents no more than a convenient set of labels. In the surplus approach, however, there is substance behind the designations. Agents of different classes are assumed to have different behaviour patterns. For example, the consumption and savings behaviour of workers is assumed to be different from that of capitalists. These differences can greatly affect the operation of the system and, consequently, are by no means of tangential relevance. Explicit sociological data are brought in, therefore, at the ground floor in this type of economics. The significance of this should be stressed. It allows economic analysis to be more easily connected with other areas of social theory and with historical changes in social structure.

Capitalist economies have generated immense economic changes and this poses great problems for analysis. Economists within the surplus approach have sought to make their subject more tractable by concentrating attention on particular patterns or states exhibited in this flux. These states have been designated by various terms; for example, 'long-period' positions, 'centres of gravity' and 'equilibria' have been three terms employed. Their characteristics, however, may be more appropriately specified in terms of a 'uniformity principle'. Rates of profit and the wages of homogeneous types of labour are each assumed to be uniform between different sectors of the economy. In addition, units of the same commodity are assumed to be traded at the same price. The rationale for concentrating on states embodying these three characteristics lies in the way competition is conceived to operate. In circumstances where the uniformities are absent, capital and labour mobility will occur and persist until the non-uniformities are eradicated. States exhibiting the uniformity principle are considered, therefore, to be terminal states or gravitational centres to which a capitalist economy will tend. Thus there is a rationale for concentrating analytical attention on states where the uniformity principle holds. Other states are incredibly diverse and in all cases are transitory.

This methodology is also employed in analysing certain types of change. When an exogenously specified variable is set at a different level it will set up changes in endogenous variables. These changes will occur over time and may be very complex. With the notion of a 'gravitational centre' their total or long-term effects can be determined by concentrating on a new equilibrium which is compatible with the new level of the exogenous variable. Changes are therefore analysed by comparing different equilibria. (Supply and demand theorists use the same method and have coined the term 'comparative statics' for the approach. Those states which are considered to be equilibria by modern supply and demand theorists are not, however, defined by the uniformity principle. See Chapter 9 below.)

The determination of uniform profit rates, wages and prices has absorbed an immense amount of theoretical effort, but the methods employed in doing so exhibit persistent strands. In general, models have been constructed in which determination is segmented and sequential. A procedure adopted by Ricardo (1817) provides a good example. Sectoral outputs and technology are assumed to be given and these are shown to imply a particular pattern of land rents. When additional assumptions are made regarding the reproductive behaviour of the working class, equilibrium real wages are dependent upon the speed of capital accumulation. Given a rate of accumulation, wage rates are determined. This, in conjunction with the prevailing technology, is shown to determine a uniform rate of profit and prices. If the accumulation rate is now allowed to be variable, capitalists' savings behaviour will determine it endogenously. This can then be shown to govern changes in sectoral outputs and technology over time.

It is obvious that the whole system is interconnected. The level established for each variable depends upon the levels of others. The procedure of determining these levels does not concentrate, however, on this simultaneity. One might suppose that this reflects the primitive 'state of the arts' which then governed theory construction. But this form of procedure has proved, in fact, more durable than the analytical techniques of economics. Economists in the surplus tradition have indeed shown a marked propensity to retain a 'one problem at a time' approach.

Associated with this has been a strong preference against formalising analysis in terms of 'supply and demand' constructions. This is most notable where the focus of attention is on the determinants of profits and prices. The dominant procedure has been to construct models of an economic system in which the technology, sectoral outputs and a distribution variable is taken as given. The values for uniform prices and remaining distributional variables are then shown to be determined. No explicit reference is made to the balance of supplies and demands in the determination of these values. This means that the structure of causation is different from the typical models generated by the tradition of supply and demand analysis. The theorists with which we are presently concerned have been suspicious of the logical coherence and empirical relevance of 'supply and demand' formulations. As one would suspect, this represents a source of tension between the two approaches, and we shall consider the issues involved later in Part IV.

Plan of Part II

The two preceding sections have sketched the perspectives which underlie the surplus analysis of profit. In subsequent chapters we concentrate on the three giants of this tradition: Ricardo, Marx and Sraffa. This by no means exhausts the work of this field. Although the surplus tradition has a minority status in terms of the overall development of economic analysis, there are many other theorists whose work could be considered. Mercantilist pamphleteers,[2] the French Physiocrats[3] and Adam Smith (1776) analysed the surplus prior to Ricardo. Non-Marxian socialists,[4] Dmitriev (1898) and Bortkiewicz (1907) carried out useful work in the tracks left by Ricardo and Marx. In the twentieth century the input—output analysis of Leontief and, more particularly, that of von Neumann (1937) has been extensively used by modern theorists of the surplus. All of this work, however, is not central for understanding the basic directions of the surplus approach to profit and will not be the subject of systematic treatment.

Chapters 3, 4 and 5 consider the principal theorists in turn. The purpose of these chapters is expository and any criticism which is made has been framed to aid this exposition. Criticism carrying more weight is developed in Chapters 6 and 7, where the work of Ricardo and Marx is evaluated in terms of results developed by Sraffa (1960), the most refined product of the surplus approach yet to appear. Chapter 8 concludes Part II with an outline of post-Sraffian developments. However, theories of profit based upon the analysis of surplus reappear in Parts IV and V, where they are considered in relation to supply and demand theory and the theory of effective demand.

Notes to Chapter 2

1. See, for example, Howard and King (1976, part 2).
2. See Marx (1862a).
3. See Meek (1962).
4. See Marx (1862c).

3
Classical Analysis of Surplus and Profit

Early Work

Economists began to concentrate attention on the surplus in the eighteenth century. Mercantilist and Physiocratic writers formulated various notions and used them in their analysis to make recommendations regarding the conduct of economic policy.[1] It was not, however, until Ricardo's work in the early nineteenth century that the conception of surplus became the cornerstone of a theory of profits. Smith (1776) most certainly laid important foundations for this development but his overall treatment of profit was muddled.[2] It was left to Ricardo (1817) to disentangle those strands in Smith which could be formulated into a theory of profit based squarely on a concept of surplus.

Ricardo's Theory of Profit : An Overview

Ricardo was primarily concerned with understanding capitalist development. His conception of capitalism was constituted by a model comprised of three classes, in which all transactions were via market exchange. Landlords owned land and received rents from leasing this natural resource to capitalist farmers. Homogeneous workers[3] provided labour services to capitalists in exchange for wages. Capitalists provided capital which employed labour, land and other inputs in production.

Development was seen to result primarily from enlargement of capital. Accumulation was made dependent on the size of the surplus, defined as the aggregate of all rents and profits. Wages were assumed to be close to subsistence levels,[4] owing to the operation of a population mechanism made famous by Malthus (1803). If wages were higher than subsistence, population expansion would accelerate, leading to a tendency for wages to decline in subsequent periods. If wages were below subsistence, population growth would fall, again ensuring a movement of wages back to the subsistence level. As a consequence, it was logical for Ricardo to assume that no disposable resources were incorporated in wage payments and surplus consisted of property incomes alone.

The two elements of surplus were not of equal significance in the accumulation process. Landlords were assumed to consume the bulk of their rents. Only capitalists had a high savings propensity and Ricardo assumes that savings are always invested.[5] The determinants of capitalist profits therefore became of crucial importance for the understanding of capitalist development. Moreover, the determinants of the rate of profit upon capital — the ratio of profits to the value of capital — was considered to be of special importance. The savings propensity of the capitalist class was assumed to be a relatively stable function of this rate. Thus, once the rate of profit was determined, so too was the rate of accumulation and the trajectory of capitalist development.

Ricardo located the ultimate determinant of the rate of profit in the degree of labour productivity of particular sectors of the economy. Agriculture was regarded of prime importance. It was assumed to be subject to diminishing returns. Higher levels of production required the utilisation of decreasingly fertile land. Consequently, capital accumulation, which in Ricardo's scheme was associated with increased employment of labour and population growth, would reduce labour productivity in agriculture. This in turn would result in the prices of agricultural commodities rising relative to those of manufactures. Since agricultural components figure prominently in workers' consumption requirements, this raises the value of the subsistence wage in terms of manufactures and reduces the rate of profit in the economy as a whole. Capital accumulation therefore declines and slows down the growth process.[6]

This vision of capitalist development forms an interconnected series of relationships. However, in his formal analysis, Ricardo did not attempt to establish them *in toto* by developing a model incorporating simultaneous determination. Instead, he examined one set of relationships at a time while holding all others in abeyance (see pp. 13–14). This can be illustrated by examining how he sought to alleviate the analysis of the profit rate from complications associated with the existence of land rents.

Getting 'Rid of Rent'

The crux of Ricardo's argument is as follows.[7] Assume there is a capitalist economy producing a specified set of outputs, from a given set of inputs, during some period of time. Let this economy be considered in equilibrium, where the rate of profit, wages and commodity prices are uniform. Also assume that there is a single agricultural good that is produced on two types of land which differ only in their fertility. Although only these two qualities of land are in cultivation, it is assumed that there exists an abundant supply of a third quality of land whose fertility is marginally less than the least fertile land presently utilised. On all types of land agricultural production requires fixed quantities of inputs.

In these circumstances the least fertile land in cultivation would generate no rents for landlords. The value of output from such land would be only sufficient to cover the cost of inputs and pay profits at the prevailing rate. If landlords sought to charge farmers rent for this land, these farmers would cease to utilise it. Instead, they would produce on the third-quality land. Since this is in excess supply, competition would ensure that its rental price is zero. Therefore, the least fertile land in cultivation can generate no rent.

The land of highest quality would be hired by capitalists at a rent equal in value to the higher output associated with its greater fertility. If rent were below this level, capitalists would make higher profits in the cultivation of this land compared with the profits received on the 'no-rent' land. Competition would ensure that landlords receive a rent equal in value to the increased output generated on the best land.

The model can easily be extended to cover the case of many qualities of land. Analogous arguments to those used above show that the pattern of land rents would reflect differential fertilities.

Once outputs are specified, the least fertile land in cultivation is determined. Equilibrium prices, consistent with a uniform rate of profit, must be such as to allow the payment of all costs and receipt of profit, at the uniform rate, in all activities. This includes production on the least fertile land in cultivation. Equilibrium prices are not affected, therefore, by rents associated with this land, for there are no rents. Furthermore, the rents of more fertile land are determined by differential fertilities, which are factors purely internal to the agricultural sector. They are no more than an aspect of agricultural technology. Consequently, positive land rents reflect, rather than determine, equilibrium prices. They reflect, therefore, rather than determine, the uniform rate of profit incorporated in equilibrium prices. Thus, for the purpose of analysing the determinants of prices and profits, it can be assumed that *all* agricultural production takes place on the no-rent land. Although this is not actually the case, the 'unreal' assumption does not distort the conclusions.

The Inverse Relation Between the *Numéraire* Wage and the Rate of Profit

In order to support his theory of capitalist development (outlined on pp. 17–19), Ricardo believed he needed to establish an inverse relation between the money wage and rate of profit. The process of accumulation would not alter the equilibrium level of the real wage – the subsistence commodity bundle. However, by requiring successively less fertile land to be brought into cultivation, accumulation would be associated with a rise in agricultural prices. This would lead to a rise in the money wage required to purchase subsistence requirements. According to Ricardo, it was precisely this increase in

the money wage which would be responsible for a decline in
the profit rate. He was obliged, therefore, to justify his con-
tention.

Before proceeding to consider Ricardo's analysis of this
issue, we should first clarify what the term 'money wage'
means. Ricardo conceives of money as a produced commodity
and in the circumstances of the time we would naturally think
that gold would be the appropriate choice. However, from a
purely analytical perspective, the choice of which commodity
should be chosen as money is open. For example, it could be
green beans, bananas or a unit of labour. Measuring prices
and 'money wages' in such a way is usually indicated by referring to the chosen commodity as a '*numéraire*'. This terminology will be adopted here.

The profit associated with any production activity is the
difference between the value of outputs and production costs.
Any change in the *numéraire* wage may change not only costs
of production but also the equilibrium prices of all outputs.
It is therefore no surprise that Ricardo believed he needed a
theory of value in order to assess the bearing which any such
price changes had on profits.

Ricardo initially adopted a labour theory of value. According to this theory, the ratio of equilibrium prices for any two
commodities would equal the ratio of the corresponding
quantities of labour required for their production. These
'embodied labour' coefficients include the 'direct' labour
utilised, together with the 'indirect' labour embodied in the
required means of production. For example, if a unit of commodity x can be produced with one unit of direct labour and
one unit of coal, and the coal requires one unit of labour to
be produced, then commodity x has a 'labour value', or
'embodied labour coefficient', equal to 2.0.

Smith (1776, pp. 53–5) had jettisoned such an approach
to value, on the grounds that the existence of private property
in land and capital necessarily invalidates it. He reasoned that
in these circumstances prices would have to be sufficiently
high to cover property incomes in addition to labour costs
and, consequently, relative prices would deviate from ratios
of embodied labour. Ricardo attempted to show that Smith
was incorrect in this belief. He utilised his theory of rent to

prove that the existence of rents were without relevance to price determination. Furthermore, Ricardo argued, provided the different forms of fixed and circulating capital were used in the same proportions in all sectors, the existence of profit, when allocated on the basis of a uniform rate, was not incompatible with the labour theory. When 'constitutions of capital' are equal, every sector utilises each type of capital in the same proportion to direct labour. Consequently, the indirect labour component in every sector bears the same proportion to direct labour. Therefore, relative equilibrium prices must equal corresponding ratios of embodied labour coefficients. The existence of profits is immaterial (see also pp. 29–30).

On the basis of the labour theory of value, Ricardo could provide an exact proof of the inverse relation between the *numéraire* wage and the profit rate. Aggregate profits are inversely related to the 'proportion of the annual labour . . . directed to the support of the labourers'.[8] When the *numéraire* wage increases, this proportion rises and profits fall. An increase in the *numéraire* wage will not change any price since the labour theory of value holds. Therefore, the value of non-wage capital is constant and the value of wage capital rises. This means the rate of profit must fall.

This argument can be extended to incorporate a decline in agricultural productivity. Such a decline means the value of the subsistence wage increases and profits fall. The rate of profit will also fall. The increase in agricultural unit labour costs cannot reduce the equilibrium price of any commodity, it can only raise them. Thus the prices of capital goods cannot fall and the ratio of profits to the value of capital – the rate of profit – must decline.

Ricardo generalised this conclusion somewhat. He maintained that the rate of profit was determined exclusively by the conditions of production in wage-good industries. These are the industries whose outputs entered the subsistence bundle consumed by workers. They are comprised of those sectors which produce consumption goods required by workers and, also, those sectors which provide means of production to these consumption-good industries. A reduction in the productivity of *any* wage-good industry, not just agriculture, would reduce the rate of profit. The conditions of production in all other industries, the 'luxury' industries, are irrelevant. Any change in productivity of these sectors would change 'luxury' prices but have no effect on the overall rate of profit (on this see also pp. 48–9).

Complications

Any conclusion based upon the restrictive assumptions underlying the labour theory of value is of limited relevance. Ricardo sought to generalise his analysis by considering the case where 'constitutions of capital' were unequal. But the complications of doing so proved beyond his analytical capabilities. With unequal 'constitutions of capital', a rise in the *numéraire* wage can generate complex changes in the prices of all commodities. Some may rise, some may fall, some may be unaffected. The overall effect on the rate of profit therefore becomes unclear. Moreover, Ricardo correctly perceived that both the direction and magnitude of any price movements, accompanying a change in the *numéraire* wage, depend on the *numéraire* chosen.

Ricardo drew two conclusions from his analysis of these complications. First, he retained his belief that there were definite relationships between productivity changes, price changes, changes in the wage and movements in the rate of profit. As a consequence, he thought it must be possible to choose a *numéraire*, or *numéraires*, which would clearly establish these relationships in all cases. He referred to the task of finding such units of measurement as locating an 'invariable standard of value'.[9] He worked on it unsuccessfully until the end of his life. Second, he argued that while differing 'constitutions of capital' ensured that relative equilibrium prices no longer exactly equalled ratios of embodied labour, nevertheless the deviations were quantitatively unimportant. The conclusions derived from assuming the labour theory of value to be strictly valid were not incorrect in essentials.[10]

Ricardianism

Ricardo's theoretical work on profit remained incomplete.
He never succeeded in providing a logical foundation outside
of a context in which the labour theory of value held exactly.
Consequently, he had to content himself with 'patching up
his argument as best he could'.[11] This was a major reason
why Ricardo's theory of profit was quickly jettisoned by
other economists.[12] Another reason for this eclipse was non-
analytic. Ricardo's ideas were increasingly interpreted to
support radical social change. His own ideology was unsullied
liberalism. Ricardo designed his analysis of profit to attack
those institutions which he considered to be impediments to
capitalist accumulation. In particular, he sought to demonstrate the inexpediency of any restrictions upon international
trade. Domestic protection, by increasing the labour cost of
wage goods, could only act to reduce the rate of profit, and
thus slow down accumulation of capital. However, Ricardo's
investigations into the labour theory of value were later utilised
by socialist reformers. They argued that this theory implied
that workers 'should' receive the surplus.[13]

For both reasons economists increasingly favoured a supply
and demand framework of analysis, and a utility theory of
choice which was believed to underlie both 'demands' and
'supplies'. In the nineteenth century Marx was 'Ricardo's
only great follower'.[14]

Notes to Chapter 3

1. See Schumpeter (1954), Meek (1962), Walsh and Gram (1980),
   and Bradley and Howard (1982a).
2. See Dobb (1973, pp. 38—64).
3. Ricardo did not assume explicitly homogeneous labour but he
   believed there were no major problems involved in aggregating
   heterogeneous labour.
4. Ricardo allows culturally defined standards to influence the level
   of subsistence.
5. See Garegnani (1978a).
6. Ricardo (1817, pp. 120—1).

7. This section is a very simplified treatment of Ricardo's argument. The rationale for the simplifications employed is not solely expository. See the first section of Chapter 6.
8. Ricardo (1817, p. 49).
9. See Bradley and Howard (1982b).
10. See Stigler (1958).
11. Robinson and Eatwell (1973, p. 22).
12. Schumpeter (1954, part 3).
13. See Meek (1967, pp. 51–74), Dobb (1973, pp. 96–120), and Meek (1977, pp. 149–64).
14. Schumpeter (1954, p. 596).

4

Marxian Analysis of Surplus and Profit

Surplus and Historical Development

Marx's analysis of the surplus is more ambitious than that of any other work with which we shall be concerned. The surplus concept forms the basis of a comprehensive social theory, encompassing all historical development. Social relationships, for Marx, are essentially those of classes, and at the centre of any class society are the relationships through which the dominant classes extract and gain control of the surplus. This is the case whether the historical form is that of oriental despotism, slavery, feudalism or capitalism:

> The specific economic form, in which . . . surplus . . . is pumped out of direct producers, determines the relationship of rulers and ruled, as it grows directly out of production itself and, in turn, reacts upon it as a determining element. Upon this, however, is founded the entire formation of the economic community which grows up out of the production relations themselves, thereby simultaneously its specific political form. It is always the direct relationship of the owners of the conditions of production to the direct producers — a relation always naturally corresponding to a definite stage in the development of the methods of labour and thereby its social productivity — which reveals the innermost secret, the hidden basis of the entire social struc-

ture and with it the political form of the relation of sovereignty and dependence, in short, the corresponding specific form of the state.[1]

Capitalism is characterised by the specific mode through which the property-owning classes appropriate the surplus, in the form of profits and rents. In *Capital*[2] Marx sought to delineate how this operated, and formulated a theory in which all property incomes represented the exploited labour of the working class. Moreover, Marx maintained that the entire pattern of capitalist development took its character from this phenomenon of exploitation.

The methodology which Marx used to accomplish this, is in many ways, unique.[3] However, through the analysis of profit there runs a strong Ricardian influence. Here the method is one of equilibrium analysis, with equilibrium defined in terms of the uniformity principle (see p. 13), in a context of exogenously specified outputs. Moreover, his analysis of the profit rate over time rests upon and is expounded in terms of the comparison of such equilibria. The presentation of the theory is, however, very unRicardian. Marx concentrated upon a pure capitalist economy in which scarce land is absent. This, together with other complications, is brought in at a much later stage, and the profit theory was modified in consequence. We shall not be concerned with these complicating factors and instead shall focus wholly on the more abstract theory, which is clearly of prime importance. In doing so we shall also utilise some simplifying assumptions which Marx did not explicitly make. Throughout this chapter labour is assumed to be homogeneous, to be paid in advance of outputs, and all capital is assumed to be circulating capital, which completely depreciates over the period of production. These are important assumptions and their significance will be considered later (in Chapter 7). In addition, our treatment of Marxian theory will extend somewhat beyond Marx. His own analysis in certain important respects has a provisional air to it. These areas have been reworked and polished by later theorists and, consequently, it is they who more clearly reveal the logical relations involved in Marx's own treatment.

Profit as Exploited Labour

Marx explicitly defines the *value* of a commodity as its embodied labour content. It is a distinct category from that of equilibrium price or, in Marx's terminology, 'price of production'. This is in contrast with Ricardo, who most frequently identified value with price. On the basis of this distinction, Marx's theory of profit is essentially concerned with the problem of how equilibrium prices may be derived from values, and thus how profit, which appears as a difference between prices, may be considered to be a magnitude of labour value.

Marx classifies the labour value of any commodity into three components, which he calls constant capital (c); variable capital (v) and surplus value (s). Constant capital is the value of indirect labour, or, put alternatively, the labour value of the physical means of production 'used up' in the production of the commodity. Variable capital is the value of direct labour services, or, in Marx's terminology, the 'value of labour power'. It is represented by the labour value of the commodities present in the wage bill advanced to produce the commodity. The remaining or residual component is surplus value. Given the way constant and variable capital are defined, the surplus value must represent the value created by direct labour, over and above the values received in the form of wages. Surplus value, therefore, is exploited labour and Marx refers to the ratio of surplus value over variable capital as the 'rate of exploitation' or 'rate of surplus value'. Assuming that wages are uniform, this ratio must also be uniform between different sectors of the economy.

Marx considers the problem of why, in the equilibrium of a capitalist economy, surplus value should be positive. Formally, but not substantively, his argument is the same as that which Ricardo would have given to explain why equilibrium wage payments failed to encroach on the surplus: namely, there are forces operating to keep wages at a subsistence level, which is less than average labour productivity. Marx argued against the Malthusian population principle, but maintained that technical change operated in capitalism so as to ensure sufficient unemployment which drove down wages to a subsistence level. (As with Ricardo, subsistence includes culturally defined elements.)

Let us assume that the economy is composed of only three sectors, each of which produces a single output: department I, which produces constant capital; department II, which produces the commodities consumed by workers; and department III, which produces 'luxuries'. It can be represented in value form as:

$$
\left.
\begin{array}{lll}
\text{Department I} & c_1 + v_1 + s_1 = v_1^* \\[2mm]
\text{Department II} & c_2 + v_2 + s_2 = v_2^* \\[2mm]
\text{Department III} & c_3 + v_3 + s_3 = v_3^*
\end{array}
\right\} \qquad (4.1)
$$

The assumption that the economy is composed of only three departments is not a significant assumption for any of the results discussed in this chapter. However, the assumption that each department only produces a single output is more fundamental, as we shall subsequently see in Chapter 7. The subscripts on the cs, vs and ss refer to departments and $v_i^*(i = 1, \ldots, 3)$ denote total outputs, measured in labour value. Throughout *Capital*, until part 2 of volume III, Marx assumes that the labour theory of value is valid. Consequently, the ratios of equilibrium prices equal the corresponding ratios of embodied labour coefficients. Further, if a unit of embodied labour is taken as the *numéraire*, equilibrium prices will equal corresponding labour values, while the profit in each department will equal the surplus value generated in that department. The equilibrium rate of profit in each sector will be equal to $s_i/(c_i + v_i)(i = 1, \ldots, 3)$, and these will equal

$$
\sum_i s_i / \sum_i (c_i + v_i)
$$

Dividing through by the appropriate v, these formulae can be written as $e/k_i + 1$ ($i = 1, \ldots, 3$) and $e/k + 1$, where e is the (uniform) rate of exploitation, k_i is the 'organic composition of capital (c_i/v_i) in department $i(i = 1, \ldots, 3)$ and k is the system-wide 'organic composition' $\sum_i(c_i/v_i)$.

Like Ricardo, Marx was aware that the labour theory of value rested on stringent assumptions. In terms of Marxian categories, Ricardo's equal 'constitutions of capital' become equal 'organic compositions' of capital, and we can see from Marx's formulae that with such an equality rates of profit are the same between sectors. Thus, in this case, the labour theory of value is compatible with uniform prices involving uniform rates of profit. Unlike Ricardo, however, Marx did not assume that the labour theory of value gave approximately correct results for equilibrium prices and profits, if the precise conditions for its validity were not met. The reasons he utilised the labour theory of value so extensively were very different.[4]

One such reason was that Marx believed he could show that even when sectoral organic compositions of capital were unequal, three 'system-wide' or aggregate relationships, derived from the labour theory of value, retained validity. These three relationships were:

(a)   aggregate surplus value equalled aggregate profits,
(b)   aggregate outputs measured in labour values equalled aggregate output measured in prices of production, and
(c)   the uniform rate of profit was equal to $e/(k + 1)$.

Following Seton (1957) we call these three relationships 'invariance postulates'. Consequently, Marx believed that his analysis of capitalism *as a system*, or at the aggregate level, carried out on the basis of the labour theory of value, was not sensitive to relaxing this assumption. In parts 1 and 2 of volume III of *Capital* Marx sought to justify these propositions, by transforming surplus value into profit, and values into prices of production.

Marx's Transformation Procedure

Marx sought to carry out this transformation, by showing that once the value system, as represented in equations (4.1), was assumed known, prices of production and the uniform rate of profit would be determined at levels which incorporated the three invariance postulates. His transformation procedure can be represented by the following equations:[5]

Department I $(c_1 + v_1)(1 + r) = v_1^* p_1^*$

Department II $(c_2 + v_2)(1 + r) = v_2^* p_2^*$

Department III $(c_3 + v_3)(1 + r) = v_3^* p_3^*$

$$r = \sum_i s_i / \sum_i (c_i + v_i)$$

$$(4.2)$$

The c_i, v_i, s_i and v_i^* are defined as before, r represents the uniform rate of profit and $p_i^* (i = 1, \ldots, 3)$ are price–value ratios. These ratios convert economic quantities measured in labour values into corresponding economic quantities measured in equilibrium prices. Each department's output, measured in equilibrium prices $(v_i^* p_i^*; i = 1, \ldots, 3)$, is consistent with an equal rate of profit, recovers the requisite wage bill $(v_i, i = 1, \ldots, 3)$ and incorporates depreciations of capital $(c_i; i = 1, \ldots, 3)$. The four equations in (4.2) allow the endogenous variables, or unknowns $(p_i; i = 1, \ldots, 3; r)$, to be expressed in terms of the exogenous data $(c_i, v_i$ and $s_i; i = 1, \ldots, 3)$. Moreover, Marx's three invariance postulates are all satisfied; $r = e/(k + 1)$ directly by the fourth equation, and all four equations together, will ensure that aggregate surplus value is equal to aggregate profits, $(\Sigma_i s_i = r \Sigma_i (c_i + v_i))$, and that aggregate output is the same whether measured in labour values, or prices $(\Sigma_i v_i^* = \Sigma_i v_i^* p_i^*)$.[6] On this basis, Marx maintains that only a redistribution of surplus value is involved in the transformation. But it is this which explains, in his view, the deceptive 'appearances' created by capitalist relations of production, and the development of erroneous 'vulgar' theories attributing profit to the productivity of capital:

> It is then only an accident if the surplus value, and thus the profit, actually produced in any particular sphere of production, coincides with the profit contained in the selling price of a commodity . . . At a given degree of exploitation, the mass of surplus value produced in a particular sphere of production is then more important for the aggregate average profit of social capital, and thus for

the capitalist class in general, than for the individual capitalist in any specific branch of production. It is of importance to the latter only insofar as the quantity of surplus value produced in his branch helps to regulate the average profit. But this is a process which occurs behind his back, one he does not see, nor understand, and which indeed does not interest him. The actual difference of magnitude between profit and surplus-value — not merely between the rate of profit and the rate of surplus-value — in the various spheres of production now completely conceals the true nature and origin of profit not only from the capitalist, who has a special interest in deceiving himself on this score, but also from the labourer.[7]

The labour theory of value is therefore, on Marx's argument, essential to the scientific understanding of profit and prices: 'If one did not take the definition of value as the basis, the *average profit*, and therefore also the [prices of production], would be purely imaginary and untenable. Without . . . [the determination of value by labour] . . . the average profit is an average of nothing, pure fancy.'[8] In Meek's words, surplus value provides a 'prior concrete magnitude' determining profit, 'a magnitude independent of market prices which could plausibly be regarded as constituting the ultimate source of profit'.[9]

Other Transformation Procedures

Marx realised, however, that his transformation procedure was inadequate.[10] Equations (4.2) do not typify correctly the price and profit structure of a capitalist economy in equilibrium. The rate of profit which is equalised in such an equilibrium is the rate upon capital measured in equilibrium prices. The rate of profit in equations (4.2) is a rate upon capital measured in labour values. Consequently, the solution for $p_i^*(i = 1, . . . , 3)$ and r will not be appropriate. Marx brushed aside this problem in the most cavalier of fashions. However, formulating a transformation procedure which is not open to this objection is relatively easy. It was first done by Bortkiewicz (1907) and greatly improved by Seton

(1957).[11] Let us consider its main qualities in terms of the three-sector model we have so far used.

The procedure for transformation can be represented in the following equations:

$$
\left.
\begin{aligned}
(c_1 p_1^* + v_1 p_2^*)(1 + r) &= v_1^* p_1^* \\
(c_2 p_1^* + v_2 p_2^*)(1 + r) &= v_2^* p_2^* \\
(c_3 p_1^* + v_3 p_2^*)(1 + r) &= v_3^* p_3^* \\
p_3 &= 1
\end{aligned}
\right\}
\tag{4.3}
$$

As can be seen, capital inputs $(c_i, v_i; i = 1, \ldots, 3)$ are now transformed into prices as well as outputs. Marx's fourth equation, which determines the rate of profit directly, is dropped and an equation explicitly stating the units in which prices are measured is added.[12] This equation thus defines the *numéraire* as a unit of embodied labour in department III. The equations represented in (4.3) can be used to solve for the endogenous variables $(p_i; i = 1, \ldots, 3; r)$ in terms of the exogenous value data $(c_i, v_i, v_i^*, i = 1, \ldots, 3)$.[13] In Marx's terms, values may be transformed into 'prices of production', and surplus value into profits.

From Marx's own perspective this transformation procedure is, however, problematic. This is because it is impossible, except in special cases, to satisfy simultaneously all three invariance postulates. As a result, there has been a long debate concerning which postulate is of most importance.[14] We can ignore this issue for two reasons. First, so far as the determination of equilibrium profits and prices is concerned, there is no problem. Labour values and prices of production are different categories. No specific unit of measurement suggests itself naturally for either. Consequently, there is no analytical substance in any equality or inequality between surplus values and profits, or in any equality or inequality between outputs measured in values or prices. Furthermore, since the rate of profit is an endogenous variable, determined simultaneously with prices of production, there is no reason to expect that it will bear any simple relation to the labour-value data, such as that incorporated in Marx's formula, $r = e/(k + 1)$. Marx, of course, seemed to take a contrary view. But there is no reason to take his view as privileged in any analytic sense. Moreover, although Marx based much of his analysis of the 'laws of motion' of capitalist development on the three conditions discussed, there is no reason to expect *on this ground alone* that the substance of his analysis, thereby, was faulted. (The causal mechanisms he specified could still be valid. As will be seen in Chapter 6, they are not, but this has nothing to do with invariance postulates.) Second, the essence of Marx's exploitation theory of profits, i.e. that surplus value is the source of profits, can be established independently of the status of the 'invariance postulates'. On the assumptions that have governed our treatment of Marx's theory (see pp. 27, 29), Morishima and others have proved that positive surplus value (or a positive rate of exploitation) is a necessary and sufficient condition for positive profits (or a positive rate of profit). This is called, rather aptly, the *fundamental Marxian theorem*.[15] One implication of the theorem is that *any* model of a capitalist economy which involves positive profits must be one in which there is exploitation in Marx's sense. This is so, whether or not the model is explicitly constructed in terms of Marx's categories.

The Falling Rate of Profit

Marx discusses the tendency of the rate of profit to fall immediately after his analysis of transformation.[16] Consequently, he felt justified in using the formula $r = \Sigma_i s_i / \Sigma_i (c_i + v_i)$. We have seen, however, that Marx's transformation procedure is inadequate, and moreover that the rate of profit cannot in general be so represented.

There is therefore a major problem associated with Marx's theory which is quite independent of the analysis he provided. Chapter 6 returns to this issue. Here we assume that conditions are such as to ensure that Marx's formula is valid. (A sufficient condition for this would be the validity of the labour theory of value.)

Dividing through by $\Sigma_i v_i$, $r = e/(k + 1)$, where e is the rate of exploitation and k the aggregate organic composition of capital. Marx argues that the labour-saving bias inherent in technical change will increase k. With a given subsistence wage this will necessarily raise e but Marx argues that e will, after some point, increase less rapidly than k, so that r will fall.[17] 'Counteracting influences' are recognised,[18] but are considered secondary.[19]

After Marx

The section above on other transformation procedures represents in a condensed form the major developments in Marxian profit theory. There have been extensions of Marxian economics beyond those considered, but none of these relates to the pure theory of profit in a closed capitalist economy, and so all of them are therefore of secondary relevance.

The Marxian theory of profit has obvious emotive connotations, and Marxism has become the theory associated with many working-class political parties. Both these factors reinforced the theoretical trend which was noted in the last section of the previous chapter. However, there were also analytic reasons for economists jettisoning the surplus approach. As with Ricardo, we have seen that Marx's work suffered from theoretical deficiencies. There are also other limitations which supply and demand theory highlight (see Chapter 15). Consequently, analytic and non-analytic forces jointly operated to keep dynamism in supply and demand theory, rather than in the surplus approach.

The revival of the surplus approach as an ongoing concern can be attributed directly to the work of Sraffa (1960). To be sure, supply and demand theory remains dominant, but it is not so secure as it once was, and most certainly Sraffa has breathed new life into the surplus tradition.

Notes to Chapter 4

1. Marx (1894), p. 791.
2. Marx (1867), (1885) and (1894).
3. See Howard and King (1975, chs 1, 2).
4. See Bradley and Howard (1982b).

36   *Profit in Surplus Theory*

5. Marx (1894, pp. 155–7).
6. See Howard and King (1975, chs 4, 5).
7. Marx (1894, pp. 167–8).
8. Marx (1862b, p. 190).
9. Meek (1977, p. 176).
10. Marx (1894, p. 161).
11. See also Dmitriev (1898).
12. In formulating his transformation algorithm Marx did not explicitly measure prices in terms of labour to compare them with labour values. Instead, he normalised prices so that the costs of production, other than profit costs, remained unaffected by the transformation. Such a procedure is valid only under very special conditions. See Morishima (1973, ch. 7) and Shaikh (1977).
13. Bortkiewicz (1907, pp. 202–3). Assuming stationary conditions, i.e. no accumulation, the solutions are as follows. Defining $f_i = v_i/c_i$ and $g_i = (c_i + v_i + s_i)/c_i$, $(i = 1, \ldots, 3)$:

$$p_1^* = \frac{f_1 p_2^*(1 + r)}{g_1 - (1 + r)}$$

$$p_2^* = \frac{g_3}{g_2 + (f_3 - f_2)(1 + r)}$$

$$r = \frac{f_2 g_1 + g_2 - \sqrt{(f_2 g_1 - g_2)^2 + 4 f_1 g_1 g_2}}{2(f_2 - f_1)} - 1$$

It is interesting to observe that neither g_3 nor f_3 appears in the solution for r. The rate of profit is therefore independent of the conditions of production in the luxury department.
14. See, for example, Sweezy (1942), Winternitz (1948), Seton (1957), Meek (1967, pp. 143–57), Laibman (1973), Howard and King (1975), Meek (1977, pp. 95–229), and King (1982).
15. Morishima (1973, p. 6). See also Morishima and Catephores (1978, p. 30).
16. Marx (1894, part 3).
17. Marx (1894, p. 305) and Marx (1857, p. 304).
18. Marx (1894, p. 232).
19. Marx (1894, pp. 236, 239).

5
Sraffa's Analysis of Surplus and Profit

The Nature and Significance of Sraffa's Work

Sraffa's *Production of Commodities by Means of Commodities* is a very dense work. The analysis is constructed in terms of exceedingly abstract models and the emphasis is placed squarely on conceptual precision and logical rigour, coupled with an economy in presentation. The significance of the work is not made explicit, but it has been seen by contemporary adherents of the surplus approach to involve a dual importance: first, as providing the basis for a thoroughgoing critique of previous economic theory and especially of that theory relating to profit – this critique includes both prior developments in the surplus approach and theories based upon 'supply and demand'; second, as laying the foundation for a 'magnificent rehabilitation' of the surplus approach to economic analysis in general and of profit in particular.[1]

This second point seems to come into conflict with the first, but this is not actually the case. Although Sraffa's work has quite devastating consequences for classical and Marxian economics, nevertheless the critique is from within the surplus perspective and methodology. Since it is an 'internal' critique, it is not the surplus approach itself which is undermined. Indeed, it is strengthened because the defects in previous work are exposed and shown to be extraneous to the surplus paradigm. Sraffa's work therefore represents a foundation on which the surplus approach can be reconstructed and so rescued from the doldrums into which it had fallen with the rise to dominance of 'supply and demand' theories.

This chapter provides a thumbnail sketch of the *Production of Commodities by Means of Commodities*. In Chapters 6 and 7 the critique of preceding surplus theory, which is embedded in the work, will be spelt out. The defects which it simultaneously exposes in supply and demand theories is the topic of Chapter 14.

The Problems Considered

Sraffa's primary concern is to examine the relationships that exist between the rate of profit, technology, relative prices and wages in particular types of economic systems which are in equilibria exhibiting the uniformity principle.

The technology of one such system studied by Sraffa can be represented as follows:

$$\left.\begin{aligned}
a_{11} + a_{12} + \ldots + a_{1n} + f_1 &\to b_1 \\
a_{21} + a_{22} + \ldots + a_{2n} + f_2 &\to b_2 \\
\cdot \quad\quad \cdot \quad\quad\quad\quad \cdot \quad\quad \cdot \\
\cdot \quad\quad \cdot \quad\quad\quad\quad \cdot \quad\quad \cdot \\
\cdot \quad\quad \cdot \quad\quad\quad\quad \cdot \quad\quad \cdot \\
a_{n1} + a_{n2} + \ldots + a_{nn} + f_n &\to b_n
\end{aligned}\right\} \tag{5.1}$$

$a_{ij}(i, j = 1, \ldots, n)$ represent the input of commodity j required in process i to produce b_i of commodity i (some a_{ij} can be zero); $f_i(i = 1, \ldots, n)$ represent the input of homogeneous labour required to produce b_i of commodity i; $b_i(i = 1, \ldots, n)$ represent the quantity of commodity i produced by these inputs.

The system in price terms is represented by the following equations:

$$\left.\begin{aligned}
(a_{11}p_1 + a_{12}p_2 + \ldots + a_{1n}p_n)\,(1+r) + f_1 w &= p_1 \\
(a_{21}p_1 + a_{22}p_2 + \ldots + a_{2n}p_n)\,(1+r) + f_2 w &= p_2 \\
\cdot \quad\quad \cdot \quad\quad\quad\quad\quad \cdot \quad\quad \cdot \quad\quad \cdot \\
\cdot \quad\quad \cdot \quad\quad\quad\quad\quad \cdot \quad\quad \cdot \quad\quad \cdot \\
\cdot \quad\quad \cdot \quad\quad\quad\quad\quad \cdot \quad\quad \cdot \quad\quad \cdot \\
(a_{n1}p_1 + a_{n2}p_2 + \ldots + a_{nn}p_n)\,(1+r) + f_n w &= p_n
\end{aligned}\right\} \tag{5.2}$$

$p_i (i = 1, \ldots, n)$ are commodity prices, r is the uniform rate of profit and w is the uniform wage; $b_i (i = 1, \ldots, n)$ do not explicitly appear because they have all been set equal to unity. Theoretically this is always possible since the units in which commodities are measured are arbitrary and can be chosen for the convenience of analysis. It should be noted, however, that Sraffa employs the same methodology as that adopted by Ricardo and Marx. Output levels are assumed to be exogenously specified and there is no suggestion that a change in outputs would leave unit input coefficients (the a_{ij}) unchanged. This would require constant returns to scale and Sraffa is explicit that no such assumption is made.[2]

In terms of this system Sraffa's usual definition of the surplus would be the quantities

$$(1 - a_{11} - a_{21} - \ldots - a_{n1}) + \ldots + (1 - a_{1n} - a_{2n} - \ldots - a_{nn})$$

Thus wage payments are included in surplus, which is therefore equivalent to net national income. However, there is no reason why the surplus could not be defined differently, to exclude wage payments (as in the work of Ricardo and Marx), or exclude those elements of wage payments which are considered to be subsistence requirements. Sraffa explicitly recognises this and adopts the practice of including wage payments in surplus only because it is more suitable for his own analysis.[3] Also, equations (5.2) imply that wages are paid at the end of the production period. No profit factor $(1 + r)$ enters into the $f_i w$ expressions. This means wage payments do not form part of capital 'advanced' prior to the date on which outputs materialise. This is in contrast with the practice of Ricardo and Marx, but again Sraffa's procedure is not imperative. It is adopted because it frequently makes analysis very much easier. (It is also not clear, *a priori*, whether it is more reasonable to assume *ex post* payment of wages or treat them as an advance.)[4]

The system represented in equations (5.2), together with other systems which are more complex, is the subject of Sraffa's analysis. In each case, answers to the following types of question are given:

1. How does the rate of profit and prices change as the wage varies?

2. How are such relationships affected by changing the
    numéraire?
3. Are there commodities whose conditions of production
    predominate in the determination of other magnitudes,
    such as the rate of profit?
4. Assuming that there are many such systems, each with a
    different technology, which system maximises the rate of
    profit for a given wage, and how does the ranking by
    profitability change with changes in the wage?

The importance of such analysis is clear for any economics
founded on the concept of surplus. As was indicated in Chapter 2 (pp. 13–14), the methodology employed concentrates
on 'centres of gravity' or equilibria, defined by the uniformity
principle. Most of the systems analysed by Sraffa are such
centres of gravity. Consequently, their properties are of the
utmost concern. Sraffa's propositions provide laws of change
applicable to the rate of profit and other magnitudes, as economies move between such equilibria.

This also allows us to understand the nature of the criticism
inherent in Sraffa's work. Many of the propositions which he
derives contradict the propositions formulated by classical
and Marxian economists. Since Sraffa's propositions are validly
deduced,[5] it follows that those of the Ricardian and Marxian
systems are flawed, or apply only under restrictive conditions.
The same method of criticism applies to supply and demand
theories. Although these theories are founded on very different principles from those underlying surplus theory (see
Chapter 9), nevertheless such theories have generated relationships contrary to those shown to be true by Sraffa. It follows
that the analytical structure, which produced a relationship
contrary to that proved in Sraffa's work, must involve error.

In Chapters 6, 7 and 14 we shall see that the critique which
can be mounted on the basis of Sraffa's analysis is impressive.
In all cases the critique is not one concerning peripheral matters. It strikes at the foundation of conceptual coherence and
logical structure of these theories. In Joan Robinson's perceptive phrase, Sraffa's work is a 'doubly-distilled elixir' that
may be savoured 'drop by drop for many a day'.[6]

Complexities

The analysis of a system represented by equations (5.2) is not simple. Sraffa's work, however, incorporates an analysis of much more complex systems than this. The most complex system dealt with includes joint-product as well as single-product processes, fixed as well as circulating capital, and the use of non-produced inputs like land as well as produced commodities. We do not need to consider explicitly such a system, but since complications associated with joint-production processes will be important in the following chapters some discussion of this is apt.

Allowing for joint production will mean considering a system whose technology is represented by (5.3):

$$\left.\begin{array}{l} a_{11} + a_{12} + \ldots + a_{1n} + f_1 \to b_{11} + b_{12} + \ldots + b_{1n} \\ a_{21} + a_{22} + \ldots + a_{2n} + f_2 \to b_{21} + b_{22} + \ldots + b_{2n} \\ \quad \cdot \qquad \cdot \qquad \qquad \cdot \qquad \cdot \qquad \cdot \qquad \qquad \cdot \\ \quad \cdot \qquad \cdot \qquad \qquad \cdot \qquad \cdot \qquad \cdot \qquad \qquad \cdot \\ \quad \cdot \qquad \cdot \qquad \qquad \cdot \qquad \cdot \qquad \cdot \qquad \qquad \cdot \\ a_{n1} + a_{n2} + \ldots + a_{nn} + f_n \to b_{n1} + b_{n2} + \ldots + b_{nn} \end{array}\right\} \quad (5.3)$$

In price terms, the system is represented as follows:

$$\left.\begin{array}{l} (a_{11}p_1 + a_{12}p_2 + \ldots + a_{1n}p_n)(1+r) + f_1 w = b_{11}p_1 + b_{12}p_2 + \ldots + b_{1n}p_n \\ (a_{21}p_1 + a_{22}p_2 + \ldots + a_{2n}p_n)(1+r) + f_2 w = b_{21}p_1 + b_{22}p_2 + \ldots + b_{2n}p_n \\ \quad \cdot \qquad \cdot \qquad \qquad \cdot \qquad \quad \cdot \qquad \cdot \qquad \cdot \qquad \qquad \cdot \\ \quad \cdot \qquad \cdot \qquad \qquad \cdot \qquad \quad \cdot \qquad \cdot \qquad \cdot \qquad \qquad \cdot \\ \quad \cdot \qquad \cdot \qquad \qquad \cdot \qquad \quad \cdot \qquad \cdot \qquad \cdot \qquad \qquad \cdot \\ (a_{n1}p_1 + a_{n2}p_2 + \ldots + a_{nn}p_n)(1+r) + f_n w = b_{n1}p_1 + b_{n2}p_2 + \ldots + b_{nn}p_n \end{array}\right\}$$

$$(5.4)$$

$b_{ij}(i, j = 1, \ldots, n)$ indicate the quantity of commodity j produced by process i. Some b_{ij} may be zero. The other notation carries the same meaning as before, except that it is no longer possible to associate the production of any commodity with a particular process.

Joint production is pervasive in any economy. The slaughter of sheep, for example, produces various types of wool, hides of different quality, blood, offal and various cuts of meat. The analysis of such phenomena is not, therefore, a subsidiary matter. Rather it is the analysis of 'single-output' processes which is limited. This point is reinforced when we realise that the only generally accepted procedure for analysing fixed capital is to utilise the joint-production framework. In other words, the proper way to deal with inputs of fixed capital is to treat them as generating joint products. Fixed capital usually depreciates with its use in production over successive periods. The value of 'depreciation allowances' will vary with prices and the rate of profit prevailing. Consequently, these allowances cannot be determined externally to the determination of prices and the rate of profit. Treating fixed capital as producing joint products is the only valid way of coming to terms with this problem.

Fixed capital inputs can be represented in terms of equations (5.4) without notational modification. The commodities which constitute fixed capital components are each treated as being different goods, the difference depending upon how many production cycles in which they have been utilised. Fixed capital inputs therefore give rise to different fixed capital outputs: different in that they are one period older. This means that some of the a_{ij} and b_{ij} can refer to elements of fixed capital.[7] When the prices of all inputs and all outputs are determined, 'depreciation allowances' can be calculated easily as a difference between prices (see pp. 132–5).

This procedure for treating fixed capital did not originate with Sraffa[8] but he does put it to novel uses, as we shall see in Chapter 6.

The Assumptions

Sraffa is much more explicit as to the assumptions which underlie his analysis than were Ricardo or Marx. We have mentioned already some of these assumptions: namely, the treatment of wages as paid *ex post*, the use of the uniformity principle, the assumption of homogeneous labour and that outputs are exogenously specified. There are, however, three other assumptions which it is important to consider.

First, in every system considered each process of production is assumed to have the same period of production between the application of inputs and the realisation of outputs. This assumption is also frequently implicit in the work of Ricardo and Marx. It is by no means as restrictive as it appears. For example, a production process extending over t periods can be divided up into t sub-processes by introducing $t - 1$ sets of intermediate inputs and $t - 1$ sets of intermediate outputs. Each sub-process can then be considered a separate process with the same period of production. No property of the economy, in which the overall process plays a part, is changed by this device.

Second, each economic system considered is assumed to be comprised of data and relationships which ensure that, given the wage, uniform prices and the rate of profit are determined.[9] Sraffa explicitly expressed this assumption by stating that in each system the number of distinct processes is equal to the number of commodities other than labour.[10] However, Sraffa recognises that this is not an adequate formulation of his assumption concerning determination.[11] We shall examine this matter in Chapter 15 but can now give an illustration for a simple system represented by:

$$\left.\begin{array}{l} a_{11}p_1(1 + r) + f_1 w = p_1 \\ a_{21}p_1(1 + r) + f_2 w = p_2 \end{array}\right\} \tag{5.5}$$

If we assume that commodity 2 is the *numéraire*, then we can derive the following.

$$r = \frac{1 - f_2 w}{a_{11} + (a_{21}f_1 - a_{11}f_2)w} - 1 \tag{5.6}$$

$$p_1 = \frac{a_{11} + (a_{21}f_1 - a_{11}f_2)w}{a_{21}} \tag{5.7}$$

Equations (5.6) and (5.7) show that, once the wage is given, the rate of profit and the price of commodity 1 are determined. The relationships shown in (5.6) can be represented geometrically (see Figure 5.1). The curvature of the line depends upon the coefficients for a_{11}, a_{21}, f_1 and f_2. The concave line in the diagram would result if

$$\frac{a_1}{f_1} > \frac{a_2}{f_2}$$

It would be convex if

$$\frac{a_1}{f_1} < \frac{a_2}{f_2}$$

and linear if

$$\frac{a_1}{f_1} = \frac{a_2}{f_2}$$

This geometry is useful for depicting a relationship between systems. If there is another system analogous to (5.5), but involving different technical coefficients $(a_{11}, a_{12}, f_1, f_2)$, its wage-profit curve could also be represented on the same diagram, as in Figure 5.2. When the wage lies between zero and w_1, system β yields the highest rate of profit. At a wage equal to w_1 both systems are equally profitable. For a wage between w_1 and w_2, system α is the more profitable. The two systems yield the same rate of profit for a wage equal to w_2.

Third, it is assumed that in every economic system there is at least one 'basic' commodity. The term 'basic' commodity has a precise meaning and the distinction from 'non-basics' is important for understanding the determination of the rate of profit. For a system represented in (5.1) and (5.2) basic com-

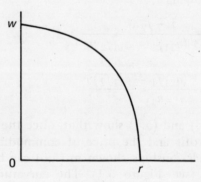

Figure 5.1

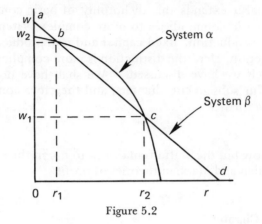

Figure 5.2

modities are those which enter, *directly or indirectly*, as means of production into all commodities. Non-basics are all other commodities. The example below illustrates the difference:

$$a_{12}p_2(1+r) + f_1 w = p_1$$
$$a_{21}p_1(1+r) + f_2 w = p_2 \tag{5.8}$$
$$a_{31}p_1(1+r) + f_3 w = p_3$$

Commodities 1 and 2 are basic. Commodity 3 is non-basic. Commodity 1 enters the production of all three commodities. It enters directly as an input into commodity 2 and commodity 3. It is indirectly utilised in the production of itself through the use of commodity 2. Similarly, commodity 2 is directly used in the production of commodity 1 and indirectly enters into the production of commodity 3, and itself, via commodity 1. Commodity 3 does not enter into the production of any commodity.

The importance of this distinction between basics and non-basics is that the production conditions of non-basics may be totally disregarded in the determination of the rate of profit and the prices of basic commodities. For example, in (5.8) we can confine our attention to the first two equations alone and, picking one of them as *numéraire*, determine r and the other price. The equations relating to non-basics only determine the prices of non-basic commodities.[12]

Sraffa also extends this dichotomy of basic commodities
and non-basic commodities to more complex systems involving joint production, fixed capital and non-produced means
of production. Here the distinction is more complicated than
that which we have discussed.[13] We shall have no need to
utilise it in subsequent chapters, and therefore consider the
matter no further.

We can now put the Sraffa framework to use in the evaluation
of Ricardian and Marxian theories of profit.

Notes to Chapter 5

1. Meek (1967, p. 101).
2. Sraffa (1960, p. v).
3. Sraffa (1960, pp. 9—10).
4. See Steedman (1977, pp. 103—5).
5. There are some exceptions. See Manara (1968) and Steedman
   (1980).
6. Robinson (1961, p. 197).
7. This description is misleading in that the procedure described converts items of fixed capital into items of circulating capital producing joint products.
8. Sraffa attributes the origin of this conceptualisation to Torrens,
   but it is usually associated with von Neumann.
9. In the case of joint-production systems, they may not be determined uniquely. Corresponding to a given wage, there may be more
   than one rate of profit and set of relative prices. See Sraffa (1960,
   p. 62).
10. Sraffa (1960, pp. 5, 7, 44, 63, 77, 78).
11. See, for example, Sraffa (1960, pp. 59, 74—5, 90—1).
12. In the system represented by (5.5) only commodity 1 is basic. The
    reason why the technical coefficients of commodity 2 enter into
    equations (5.6) and (5.7) is because commodity 2 is taken as the
    numéraire.
13. See Sraffa (1960, pp. 47, 49—52, 54—5, 74, 78), Manara (1968),
    Steedman (1980) and Pasinetti (1980b).

6

A Sraffian Critique of Classical Profit Theory

The Ricardian Theory of Rent

Ricardo sought to 'get rid' of the complications associated with rental payments in his analysis of the relations between the wage and rate of profit. An outline of this theory was given in Chapter 3, but this represents a considerable simplification of Ricardo's own treatment. The restrictive assumptions were utilised not only to make the exposition easier but also because the theory is flawed in more complex cases. In particular, if we relax the assumption that each type of land utilises the same quantities of inputs, we can see how Sraffa's analysis reveals a defect.

Let us assume that corn alone is produced by land[1] and that there are n different kinds of land in utilisation. Ignoring the rest of the economic system, and assuming no joint production or fixed capital, the corn-producing processes can be represented by the following equations:

$$\left.\begin{array}{l} (a_{11}p_1 + a_{12}p_2 + \ldots + a_{1k}p_k)\,(1 + r) + l_1 s_1 + f_1 w = c_1 p_c \\ (a_{21}p_1 + a_{22}p_2 + \ldots + a_{2k}p_k)\,(1 + r) + l_2 s_2 + f_2 w = c_2 p_c \\ \quad \cdot \qquad \cdot \qquad \cdot \qquad\quad \cdot \qquad \cdot \qquad \cdot \qquad \cdot \qquad \cdot \\ \quad \cdot \qquad \cdot \qquad \cdot \qquad\quad \cdot \qquad \cdot \qquad \cdot \qquad \cdot \qquad \cdot \\ \quad \cdot \qquad \cdot \qquad \cdot \qquad\quad \cdot \qquad \cdot \qquad \cdot \qquad \cdot \qquad \cdot \\ (a_{n1}p_1 + a_{n2}p_2 + \ldots + a_{nk}p_k)\,(1 + r) + l_n s_n + f_n w = c_n p_c \end{array}\right\} (6.1)$$

$a_{ij}(i = 1, \ldots, n; j = 1, \ldots, k)$ represent inputs of k produced commodities; $p_i(i = 1, \ldots, k)$ are the prices of the k commodities; $l_i(i = 1, \ldots, n)$ are different areas of land and $s_i(i = 1, \ldots, n)$ are their corresponding rents; $c_i(i = 1, \ldots, n)$ represent corn outputs; p_c is the price of corn, $f_i(i = 1, \ldots n)$ are the labour inputs; w is the uniform wage; and r is the uniform rate of profit.

According to Ricardian differential rent theory, one of the elements of s_i will be zero. Assume this is s_n. The other land rentals $(s_1, \ldots, s_{n-1})$ and p_c will be determined once r, w and $p_i(i = 1, \ldots, k)$ are specified. According to Sraffa's assumptions (see pp. 43–4), r and p_i will be determined by the equations of the whole economic system once the wage is specified. Equations (6.1) do not represent the complete system but only the land using production processes. Once p_i, r and w are known, however, these equations will determine $s_i(i = 1, \ldots, n - 1)$ and p_c.

Ricardo believed that the different kinds of land could be ranked by their fertility independently of prices, wages and profit rates. From this, he deduced that in the analysis of value and profit only the nth process, involving zero rent, need be considered. Sraffa shows this to be an invalid procedure: 'The order of fertility . . . is not defined independently of the rents; that order, as well as the magnitudes of rent themselves, may vary with the variation in r and w.'[2] Thus, if at one r and w, n is the 'no-rent' process, it may not remain such with a change in distribution. Such a distributional change will alter the prices of all produced commodities involved, the $p_i(i = 1, \ldots, k)$, as well as the profits and wage costs of all corn-producing processes. Consequently, assuming, in accordance with differential rent theory, that at least one $s_i(i = 1, \ldots, n)$ is zero, then rents are determined by equations (6.1), but the relative order can change with distribution. The zero-rent process is endogenous, therefore, and not susceptible to being treated as predetermined in the construction of a theory of profit.

Wage Goods, Diminishing Returns and Changes in the Rate of Profit

It was indicated in Chapter 3 (pp. 22–3) that Ricardo generalised his theory of profit by distinguishing between 'wage goods' and 'luxuries'. If we assume that joint production is absent, this distinction is straightforward. Wage goods are those which enter, directly or indirectly, into the subsistence wage bundle. Luxuries are those that do not. Ricardo maintained that the production conditions of the latter were irrelevant to the determination of the rate of profit. No matter how input productivity changed in these luxury sectors, this would have no effect upon r. Sraffa proves the correctness of this proposition, through his distinction between basics and non-basics.

The distinction between wage goods and luxuries appears not to be the same as the distinction between basics and non-basics. The former appears to be based on use, the latter on technology. However, when proper attention is paid to the different structures of the two frameworks, the distinctions are equivalent. In the Ricardian system, unlike that of Sraffa, from a technological perspective labour is a produced commodity. The inputs required to produce labour are the components of the subsistence wage bundle. Since Ricardo implicitly assumes that labour enters directly or indirectly into the production of all commodities, wage goods are necessarily basic in terms of Sraffa's distinction. Moreover, no commodity in Ricardo's system can be basic in Sraffa's sense unless it is a wage good, since labour is a produced commodity. Thus Ricardo's distinction is really a technological distinction and identical to Sraffa's when we recognise that labour is a produced commodity.[3]

Sraffa's analysis therefore shows that Ricardo's insight into the determining role of wage goods was well founded. The conditions of production of wage goods or basics, alone are of significance for the determination of the rate of profit. The conditions of production of 'luxuries', or 'non-basics', is immaterial.[4] Consequently, within Ricardo's system, it is solely diminishing returns in wage goods which are of significance, not diminishing returns in general.

On this matter, therefore, Sraffa's analysis provides powerful support for Ricardo's insight. However, this reinforcement is actually a mixed blessing. It indicates also that Ricardo's endeavours in value theory were unnecessary. Indeed, the implications of Sraffa's analysis for Ricardo's approach goes deeper than this. Ricardo need not have considered the relation between the *numéraire* wage and rate of profit in order to establish his essential thesis concerning the falling rate of profit in the face of declining agricultural productivity. These implications follow from the fact that, in the absence of joint production, not only do changes in the production conditions of basics affect the rate of profit but also that they affect it in regular ways. Decreasing productivity in the production of any basic commodity, or, in Ricardo's terms, wage goods, is necessarily associated with a decline in the rate of profit. The simplest of the Sraffa surplus systems can be used to prove this. The basic processes can be represented by the matrix equation:

$$\mathbf{A}\mathbf{p}(1 + r) = \mathbf{p} \qquad (6.2)$$

Labour inputs and subsistence wage payments are not shown explicitly but are included in the elements of **A**. The reciprocal of the profit factor $(1/1 + r)$ is the dominant eigenvalue of the matrix **A**. The dominant eigenvalue is a continuous increasing function of every element of **A**. Consequently, r is a continuous decreasing function of every element of **A**.

The Labour Theory of Value

Although Ricardo had no analytical need for a theory of value to establish his theory of profit, it is important, nevertheless, for an overall evaluation of this theory that we consider the value theory which he did develop. After all, results may be established in more than one way.

We have already seen in Chapter 3 that by utilising the labour theory of value Ricardo could show both an inverse relation between the *numéraire* wage and rate of profit and a direct relation between declining agricultural productivity and the rate of profit. However, he realised correctly that the conditions ensuring the validity of the labour theory of value were restrictive. He failed to generalise rigorously his results beyond the confines of this special case, but suggested that this omission was not of great significance, since the labour

theory of value was approximately correct under all conditions. This was a mistake and Sraffa's analysis indicates why.

To show this, we can utilise the example of the Sraffa
system represented in equations (5.5) on page 43. The labour
values of commodity 1 and commodity 2 for this system can
be computed from the equations

$$a_{11}v_1^* + f_1 = v_1^*$$
$$a_{21}v_1^* + f_2 = v_2^*$$

as $v_1^* = f_1/(1 - a_{11})$ and $v_2^* = a_{21}f_1/(1 - a_{11}) + f_2$. Given the
technical coefficients $(a_{11}, a_{21}, f_1, f_2)$ both labour values are
fixed, as is their ratio (v_1^*/v_2^*). However, from equation (5.7)
on page 43 we can see that the price of p_1 relative to p_2
(which is set equal to 1.0) generally does vary with the wage
rate. The degree of variation, for any change in w, will
depend on the technical coefficients. This indicates that the
degree of approximation afforded by the labour theory of
value depends upon the structure of technology and the prevailing wage.[5]

This point can also be used to illustrate a deeper confusion
on the part of Ricardo. It indicates that he was not clear as to
the conditions required for the labour theory of value to hold
precisely. Ricardo worked in terms of capital aggregates and,
in particular, in terms of 'fixed' and 'circulating' capital. These
are not arbitrary categories, as they are defined by different
speeds of turnover, or durability. Ricardo considered the
labour theory of value would hold precisely if commodities
were produced with equal 'constitutions of capital' (see
pp. 21--2). Except in special cases, this is incorrect. For
example, two commodities which are means of production in
the production of some third commodity may have the same
degree of durability in this function. Both will, therefore, be
classified as representing the same type of capital in Ricardo's
scheme; but their own production conditions may be very
different. In this case their prices will change in different ways
when the wage changes. A 'unit' of a particular type of capital
in Ricardo's sense, therefore, may be variously affected depending on the inputs from which it is formed. Thus the
relevant condition ensuring the validity of the labour theory

of value is not equal 'constitutions of capital' in the Ricardian sense but equal input structures.[6] Only in this case will a distributional change leave relative prices unaffected, and thus proportional to ratios of embodied labour for all levels of the wage.

Joint Production

The critical points raised in the previous sections do not depend for their validity upon the existence of joint production. They are not undermined if joint production is considered, but they do not require it. Ricardo could not avoid the complications associated with rent even if attention were limited to production systems in which each process produces a single commodity. He did not need a theory of value and he was confused as to the status of the theory of value which he did develop. However, if joint production is considered, then even more serious defects can be shown in his theory of profit and the value theory he developed to sustain it.

In a production system involving predetermined outputs, any decrease in the productivity of any process must reduce the size of the surplus. Provided this decline in productivity does not occasion a fall in the wage, it must reduce the bundle of commodities which constitute the commodity components of profit. Similarly, an increase in the *numéraire* wage, with technology and outputs unchanged, will reduce the size of aggregate profits. Nevertheless, it is not obvious that either change will reduce the rate of profit. A change in technology, or a change in the *numéraire* wage, will be associated in general with a change in prices. These prices pertain to outputs and to means of production which form capital. Consequently both the numerator (aggregate profits) and the denominator (the value of capital) of the ratio, which will define the rate of profit, will change. Sraffa's analysis of these price movements, consequent on a change in technology or a change in the *numéraire* wage shows that there is no *a priori* reason for expecting these changes to always reduce the value of this ratio.

In systems which involve only produced commodities and

no joint production, both changes will reduce, in fact, the rate of profit. We have already shown this for the case of a decline in productivity (see p. 50). It is also true that in such systems an increase in the *numéraire* wage, with technology constant, will reduce the rate of profit. This is illustrated by Figure 5.1 (p. 44), but Sraffa proves it to be a general property of all such systems and it holds irrespective of the *numéraire* in which prices and wages are measured.[7] Both results therefore support Ricardo's theory of profit, though, as we have indicated, not the procedures he utilised in developing this theory. However, Sraffa's analysis proves that neither result can be guaranteed once joint production is considered. In these cases it is possible for a decline in input productivity to be associated with an increase in the rate of profit. Consider the system

$$\mathbf{A}\mathbf{p}(1 + r) + \mathbf{f}w = \mathbf{B}\mathbf{p} \tag{6.3}$$

and assume that diminishing returns occur. We can therefore rewrite equation (6.3) as

$$\mathbf{A}(\mathbf{I} + \mathbf{k})\mathbf{p}(1 + r) + \mathbf{f}w = \mathbf{B}(\mathbf{I} + \mathbf{k})\mathbf{p} \tag{6.4}$$

where $\mathbf{k}$ is a diagonal matrix with elements k_j along the principal diagonal, all of which are non-positive and less than unity in absolute value. These elements, k_j, thus reflect a declining productivity of labour in transforming inputs into outputs.

Equation (6.4) can be rewritten as

$$\mathbf{p} = (\mathbf{I} + \mathbf{k})^{-1}(\mathbf{B} - \mathbf{A}(1 + r))^{-1}\mathbf{f}w \tag{6.5}$$

Assume, without loss of generality, that prices are measured in labour-commanded units, so that $w = 1$, and that labour is measured such that the total labour utilised is always 1. Also, define $\mathbf{w}^*$ as the row vector representing the fixed real wage bundle of commodities consumed by workers. Consequently, $\mathbf{w}^*\mathbf{p} = 1$ and (6.5) becomes

$$1 = \mathbf{w}^*(\mathbf{I} + \mathbf{k})^{-1}(\mathbf{B} - \mathbf{A}[1 + r])^{-1}\mathbf{f}$$

Diminishing returns imply that the k_j become larger in absolute value. Therefore, the elements of $(\mathbf{I} + \mathbf{k})$ become smaller and the elements of $(\mathbf{I} + \mathbf{k})^{-1}$ become larger. This will always result in a decline in r only if $(\mathbf{B} - \mathbf{A}(1 + r))^{-1}\mathbf{f}$ is an increasing vector function of r. But this cannot be assured unless $\mathbf{B} = \mathbf{I}$, which implies the absence of joint production.[8]

It is also possible for an increase in the *numéraire* wage, assuming technology is unchanged, to be associated with an increase in the rate of profit (see p. 140).[9]

The complications associated with joint production also have devastating effects for Ricardo's theory of value. Moreover, these implications are of crucial importance for Marx's theory of profit and therefore need to be considered in some detail.

Consider a Sraffa system composed of the following two production processes:

EXAMPLE 1

INPUTS

	Commodity 1	Commodity 2	Labour
Process 1	4	0	1
Process 2	0	6	1

OUTPUTS

	Commodity 1	Commodity 2
Process 1	5	1
Process 2	2	8

Labour values are given by the equations:

$$4v_1^* + 1 = 5v_1^* + v_2^*$$
$$6v_2^* + 1 = 2v_1^* + 8v_2^*$$

where $v_i^* (i = 1, 2)$ is the labour value of commodity i. In attempting to compute these labour values we end up with two inconsistent equations:

$$1 = v_1^* + v_2^*$$
$$1 = 2v_1^* + 2v_2^*$$

Consequently, labour values cannot be computed. They are indeterminate. However, this system is capable of attaining an economically meaningful equilibrium. Assuming that commodity 1 is the *numéraire* and that the real wage is one unit of commodity 2, paid in arrears, we find that $p_1 = 1$, $p_2 = 4$ and $r = 25$ per cent.

Even if we confine attention to systems where labour values are determinate, there is no assurance that they will be positive. For example, consider the Sraffa system:

EXAMPLE 2

INPUTS

	Commodity 1	Commodity 2	Labour
Process 1	4	0	1
Process 2	0	16	1

OUTPUTS

	Commodity 1	Commodity 2
Process 1	5	1
Process 2	2	20

Computation of labour values shows that $v_1^* = 1\frac{1}{2}$ and $v_2^* = -\frac{1}{2}$. Commodity 2 therefore has a negative labour value. However, the system is quite capable of attaining a non-perverse equilibrium. Assuming that commodity 1 is the *numéraire* and that the real wage is one unit of commodity 2, paid in arrears, we find that $p_1 = 1$, $p_2 = 2$ and $r = 25$ per cent.

Another 'peculiar' case is provided by the following Sraffa system:

EXAMPLE 3

INPUTS

	Commodity 1	Commodity 2	Labour
Process 1	4	0	1
Process 2	0	12	1

OUTPUTS

	Commodity 1	Commodity 2
Process 1	5	1
Process 2	2	13

Here $v_1^* = 0$ and $v_2^* = 1$, while with the same wage and *numéraire* as above $p_1 = 1$, $p_2 = \frac{2}{3}$ and $r = 25$ per cent. Sraffa does not call explicit attention to the first and third possibility, though he does to the second. Morishima (1973) and Steedman (1975) seem to have been the first to spell out the significance of negative labour values in the context of an evaluation of Marx.

Ricardo took the determinate and positive nature of labour values as self-evident. The examples just given show that he should not have done so. They also reinforce the point made earlier (p. 51), that the labour theory of value cannot be regarded, in general, as an approximately valid theory. In the first example labour values do not exist, in the second the ratio of labour values is negative while the ratio of prices is positive.

These results seem peculiar. They do so because there is a tendency to think in terms where each commodity is produced by a single process. In such a case these 'perverse' results will not occur. However, as was indicated on page 41, joint production cannot be considered to be a complicating detail of limited relevance. It is also easy to explain why these 'perverse' results occur.

With the utilisation of positive *direct* labour inputs in all processes, the labour value of the surplus must be positive, for it must equal the total of this direct labour. The surplus in example 1 is $(5 - 4) + (2 - 0) = 3$ units of commodity 1 plus $(2 - 0) + (8 - 6) = 4$ units of commodity 2. The surplus in example 2 is 3 units of commodity 1 and 5 units of commodity 2. Since the direct labour inputs in both systems are 2, each of these surpluses must have a labour value of 2. In the case where individual commodity labour values are determinate, this means that at least one commodity must have a positive labour value. However, it may not be possible in the face of joint production to allocate the labour value of the surplus between its component parts. This is the situation in the first example above, because both processes produce net outputs in the same proportions. A necessary condition for the calculation of individual labour values is that the processes produce net outputs in different proportions.

This condition holds in the second example. But in this

case process 2 is more physically productive with regard to both net outputs. Consequently, one can hypothetically transfer labour from process 1 to process 2 and obtain more of both commodities in surplus. However, this greater surplus must absorb, or embody, no more labour than that saved by reducing the operation of the least productive process. This is only possible if one commodity has a negative labour value.

In the third example, we have a situation where process 2 is more physically productive with regard to the net output of commodity 1 and has the same productivity in the production of commodity 2. It means that commodity 1 must have a zero labour value. Hypothetically transferring labour from process 1 to process 2 results in the same labour value of national income and the same physical composition, except that more of commodity 1 is produced. This implies a zero labour value for commodity 1.

It follows that all labour values will be determinate and positive only when net outputs are produced in different proportions by the different processes and when no process dominates in productivity. As we have seen, such conditions are not required to hold for an equilibrium to exist.

Conclusion

The critique of Ricardo in terms of Sraffa could be extended to cover other material involved in the Ricardian theory of profit.[10] However, enough has been discussed in the preceding sections to show that this theory suffers severely at the hands of Sraffa. We should not read too much into this, however. The preceeding sections have concentrated on the defects of Ricardian profit theory and paid scant attention to its insights.

We move on now to consider the Marxian theory of profit. Since this is built upon a Ricardian foundation, it too is severely defective.

Notes to Chapter 6

1. This is the typical Ricardian assumption; see, for example, Stigler (1952, pp. 184, 193) and Stigler (1958, p. 333).
2. Sraffa (1960, p. 75).

3. In Sraffa's analysis wage goods may be non-basic. In most models involving a surplus Sraffa considers the wage as variable and paid out of surplus (1960, pp. 9–10). This implies that the 'necessaries' of consumption are not automatically classified as 'basics'. For example, in the case where each commodity was produced by a single process, they would only be basic if they entered, directly or indirectly, as means of production into the production of all commodities other than through wage payments to labour.

4. In systems involving joint production, however, this proposition needs modification. See Steedman (1980).

5. The technology and wage operating in Ricardo's time conceivably could have been such as to provide, at worst, a 93 per cent labour theory of value. See Stigler (1958). But whether this was or was not so, Ricardo could not possibly have known. He simply did not have the information available from which to make the calculation. Moreover, the hypothetical calculations he did make were flawed (see pp. 51–2).

6. See Sraffa (1960, pp. 12–17).

7. Sraffa (1960, p. 40).

8. See Pasinetti (1977a, pp. 267–76) and Steedman (1977, pp. 175–8).

9. See also Sraffa (1960, p. 62).

10. See Howard (1981).

7
A Sraffian Critique of
Marxian Profit Theory

Labour Values and Exploitation

The role of labour values within the Ricardian scheme was that of a device used to develop a theory of profit whose central insight and defects can be considered without explicit valuation intervening. Within the framework of the Marxian theory of profit, labour values hold a more fundamental position. It is of course true that Marx emphasises more explicitly and strongly than does Ricardo the defects of the labour theory as a predictive theory of price.[1] Moreover, Marx never suggests, nor does he require, that ratios of labour values 'approximate' ratios of equilibrium prices. But this is only an indication of the more profound role that labour values play in the Marxian system. It is because Marx maintains that equilibrium profits can be expressed in terms of labour values, under all circumstances, that he has no need to retain the Ricardian features. This is why a Sraffa-based critique of Marx is so much more fundamental. The defects that the Sraffa analysis exposes in the concept of labour value extend right to the heart of the Marxian scheme in a way that they do not in the Ricardian case.

We have seen above (pp. 54—7) that for Sraffa systems involving joint production labour values may be indeterminate, negative or zero. In itself, this has no direct significance for the Marxian theory of profit, for Marx is not concerned with labour values, *per se*, but with the derived magnitudes, c, v, s, c/v, s/v and $s/(c + v)$. However, if the primary concept is inadequate, so too will be the derived concepts. And the possibility of indeterminacy, negativity and vanishing labour values do make labour values inadequate primary concepts, given Marx's purpose of demonstrating a precise relationship between exploitation and profit. Following Ricardo, Marx implicitly assumes that labour values are well-defined, non-negative magnitudes which are positive for all produced commodities. Furthermore, he is required to make such assumptions. Without them the derived labour-value magnitudes may also become undefined, vanish or be of the 'wrong sign'. In such cases Marx's proposition simply cannot be expressed, or cannot be expressed in a sensible way. The three numerical examples provided in Chapter 6 (pp. 54–6) are quite sufficient to demonstrate this.

In the first example the labour value of both commodities is undefined. It follows that all of Marx's derived value magnitudes are undefined. Consequently, all propositions made in their terms are vacuous. In the second example both labour values and all the derived magnitudes are defined ($c_1 = 6$, $c_2 = -8$, $v_1 = -\frac{1}{2}$, $v_2 = -\frac{1}{2}$, $s_1 = 1\frac{1}{2}$, $s_2 = 1\frac{1}{2}$). However, the variable capital magnitudes are of perverse sign, as is the rate of exploitation. In the third example, the surplus value generated by both processes is zero, so the rate of exploitation is also zero ($c_1 = 0$, $c_2 = 12$, $v_1 = 1$, $v_2 = 1$, $s_1 = 0$, $s_2 = 0$). These last two examples therefore show that the *fundamental Marxian theorem* (see p. 34) will not cover all cases involving joint production. Positive surplus value is not a necessary condition for positive profit and a positive rate of exploitation is not necessary for a positive rate of profit. Surplus value is therefore *not* a 'prior concrete magnitude . . . which could plausibly be regarded as constituting the ultimate source of profits'.[2]

In the second example above, the negativity of the rate of exploitation results from the negativity of variable capitals. However, it is easy to construct examples where a negative rate of surplus value results from negative surplus values. Following Sraffa,[3] Steedman (1975) was the first explicitly to point out the possibility of negative surplus value coexisting with positive profits.

The Rate of Profit

Marx's formula for the rate of profit is clearly flawed. In the first example, it cannot give a prediction; in the second example, it predicts a profit rate of -150 per cent; and in the third, a profit rate of zero. But we know that in all cases the rate of profit is 25 per cent. This indicates that Marx's formula can be incorrect with respect to both sign and magnitude. It follows that Marx's formula does not necessarily even approximate the correct rate of profit.

Marx's formula for the rate of profit is seriously flawed even in the absence of joint production. It involves the summation of surplus values, constant capitals and variable capitals over *all* processes. We know, however, that non-basics are irrelevant for the determination of the rate of profit. Marx's formula therefore, includes redundant data.

Marx's formula can be written as $e/(k + 1)$, where e is the rate of exploitation and k is the economy-wide organic composition of capital; e depends on the productive conditions in wage-good industries alone. The 'value of labour power' is determined by the labour value of the real wage. The surplus value generated by each worker is given by the difference between this and the length of the working day, which is uniform in all processes. The rate of exploitation is therefore completely independent of the non-basic sectors of the economy. However, k is not, for it is the *economy-wide* organic composition.

Even in the case where non-basic or luxury sectors are non-existent, Marx's formula is still incorrect. The rate of profit can obviously be represented as $p_s^* s^*/p_k^* k^*$, where s^* is the column vector of commodities forming profit measured in units of embodied labour (so that the elements represent surplus values), k^* is the column vector of commodities as inputs, including wage payments to workers, again measured in units of embodied labour, and p_s^* and p_k^* are row vectors of equilibrium price/value ratios. In general, the p_s^* and p_k^* will not be such that $p_s^* s^*/p_k^* k^* = i_s s^*/i_k k^*$, where i_s and i_k are row sum vectors.

In fact, Marx's procedure is deficient in a more basic way. Like Ricardo, Marx uses aggregate capital magnitudes. The non-wage elements of capital are aggregated in each process, and over different processes, into constant capital magnitudes. Similarly, elements of wage capital are aggregated into variable capitals. Such aggregation by labour values would only be permissible if the price—value coefficients of each element of constant capital were the same and if price—value ratios of each element of variable capital were the same: 'Since some commodities enter both constant and variable capital, this in effect requires that all commodities have the same price/value coefficient, i.e. the prices are proportional to values and the whole . . . problem of transformation is absent',[4] since the labour theory of value holds.

Transformation

The considerations of this chapter so far might be thought to have quite disastrous consequences for the deriving of equilibrium prices and profits from data on labour values. Indeed they do. But the implications are not as severe as might first appear. Provided labour values are determinate and non-zero, it is always possible to undertake such a transformation in terms of a Sraffa system involving only produced commodities. Neither fixed capital nor joint production have to be ruled out. Nor is it required that labour values be positive.

The units in which commodities are measured are arbitrary. It is therefore possible to take the units to be embodied labour values. The prices of a Sraffa system then become prices 'per unit of labour value' or price—value ratios. Given the wage, similarly specified in terms of labour value, and a *numéraire* for price—value ratios, the assumptions on which a Sraffa system is built indicate that a solution exists for the prices and the rate of profit. Consequently, transformation is possible.

In the case where there are negative labour values, a negative entry for inputs and outputs would occur. However, this would only indicate that an economically meaningful solution would involve the corresponding price—value ratio being non-positive. Negative labour values therefore cause no logical problems for transformation. But if labour values were undefined, or zero, a transformation would not be possible. It would not be possible to measure commodities in units of embodied labour and price—value ratios would become undefined.

In any event, the transformation procedure is clearly unnecessary. Labour values are magnitudes derived from technology. In order to compute them, technological information is required. In Sraffa's analysis, this technological information, together with the specification of the wage, is sufficient in itself to compute prices and profits. Consequently, Samuelson was perfectly correct to characterise any transformation procedure as an 'unnecessary detour'[5] from a computational or predictive viewpoint. It follows that Marx was quite wrong to assert that without working from labour values it would be impossible to calculate prices of production and the rate of profit (see above, pp. 31–2).

Technology, Labour Values and the Rate of Profit

In both the previous chapter and the preceeding sections of this chapter the processes of production in operation have been regarded as being independent of the rate of profit. Such a view is unreasonable. There will normally be different processes of production available to all sectors of the economy and those adopted will depend on profitability in a capitalist economy. As we have seen (pp. 44–5) Sraffa incorporates this into his analysis. The system or technology in operation varies with the wage or, put alternatively, it varies with the rate of profit. This implies that the 'system' from which labour values are determined will change with the rate of profit. Therefore, in these circumstances, any theory which seeks to determine the rate of profit on the basis of labour values is circular: 'The determination of the profit rate is . . . *logically prior* to any determination of value magnitudes − it is hardly surprising then, that the latter have nothing to contribute to the former.'[6]

The Theory of the Falling Rate of Profit

Marx's theory of the falling profit rate was presented in terms of his formula for the profit rate, $e/(k + 1)$. It can therefore relate only to special cases. In addition, Marx's statement of this proposition on the movement of the profit rate is essentially assertive. It rests upon the statement that the rise in the organic composition of capital will, after some point, exceed the rise in the rate of exploitation.[7] No analysis is provided indicating the conditions required for this to occur.[8] There is, however, no difficulty in showing, through Sraffa's analysis, that Marx's theory is seriously defective.

Marx's position is exactly contrary to that of Ricardo. For Ricardo it is the declining productivity of inputs which result in a falling rate of profit, given a fixed subsistence wage. For Marx, it is the rising productivity of inputs, resulting from technical progress, which leads to the falling profit rate, given the fixed subsistence wage. It follows that the same formal analysis as was used to substantiate the essentials of Ricardo's analysis undermines that of Marx, and the possible exception to the Ricardian case, resulting from joint production, provides the only salvation for Marx (see pp. 53–4).

It also follows that, outside possible exceptions stemming from joint production, if there are no Ricardian diminishing returns,[9] if the commodity composition of the wage is fixed (as assumed by Marx), and the economy closed,[10] then technological regression rather than technological progress is required to ensure a falling rate of profit. There is of course no reason for expecting such regression, especially in a capitalist economy.

Marxian Profit Theory after Sraffa

As in the treatment of Ricardo in Chapter 6, we have concentrated on defects in Marx's theory of profit rather than any insights it exhibits. Also, we have not considered the wider issues involved in Marx's social theory. The focus has been very narrow indeed, though it cannot be argued reasonably that the exploitation theory of profit is of tangential relevance to the Marxian scheme.

The Sraffian critique does *not* imply that a concept of exploitation has no relevance for the understanding of profit. What it does imply is that utilising Marx's own concept of exploitation leads to analytical pitfalls. Other concepts of exploitation, and any theories founded upon them, would obviously have to be evaluated on their own merits. Post-Sraffian work has developed some alternative concepts of exploitation and sought to relate them to profit.[11] However, in every case the new concepts play no autonomous analytic role in determining profits and prices. These can be determined directly from the technological and distributional data which are used to define the new concepts of exploitation. These concepts of exploitation, like that of Marx's own, are therefore 'complicating detours'.

Thus in general economists concerned to develop the surplus approach have sought to develop it independently of the categories utilised by Marx in his analysis of profit. However, this in no way implies that Marxian economics as a whole, or the more general social theory in which it is encased, does not inform theory construction. In many cases it is an important influence. As has been indicated on pp. 26–7, Marx provides the most comprehensive theory of the surplus yet constructed. It extends well beyond the pure theory of profit considered in this chapter, and its validity is not undermined by the defects in this theory of profit. Consequently, Marx's work remains a valuable source of material for economists working in the surplus tradition of analysis.

Notes to Chapter 7

1. Marx (1862b, ch. 10).
2. Meek (1977, p. 16).
3. Sraffa (1980, pp. 60–1).
4. Steedman (1977, p. 63).
5. Samuelson (1957; 1970; 1971).
6. Steedman (1977, p. 65). See also Morishima (1973, pp. 189–90) and Howard and King (1975, pp. 157–60).

7. The rise in the organic composition of capital is taken for granted by Marx. It should not have been. See Howard and King (1975, ch. 6) and Steedman (1977, pp. 124–5, 132–6).
8. See Howard and King (1975, pp. 205–7).
9. Rosdolsky (1956), Erlich (1967) and Güsten (1965) have suggested that Marx did supplement his argument with Ricardian elements. There seems to be some evidence for this. However, Marx's main argument certainly does not involve diminishing returns. His exposition of the falling rate of profit occurs before his discussion of land in *Capital*.
10. Marx refers to foreign trade only as a counteracting influence to the tendency of the rate of profit to fall (Marx, 1894, p. 237).
11. See Morishima (1973; 1974), Morishima and Catephores (1978), Meek (1967, pp. 161–178), Medio (1972), Eatwell (1973; 1975), Howard and King (1975, pp. 149–56), Armstrong, Glyn and Harrison (1978), Kurz (1979) and King (1982). The most important approach is probably that of Morishima. This involves a redefinition of labour value and exploitation such that a reformulated 'fundamental Marxian theorem' may be retained in the face of joint production. What Morishima calls the 'true' value of a commodity is defined as the minimum amount of labour required for its production, given all the available methods of production and not just the processes actually employed. The value of labour power is therefore, the minimum quantity of labour required to produce the commodity bundle which forms the wage. Surplus value is the difference between the total labour employed and the value of the total labour power employed. The rate of exploitation is the ratio of the former to the latter. It is proved that 'true' values cannot be negative and that a (reformulated) fundamental Marxian theorem holds even in cases involving joint production.

8

Post-Sraffian Developments in the Surplus Approach to Profits

Surplus theory is an approach to economics in general and not just to the understanding of profit. However, more than any other type of economic analysis, distribution and profits have been at the forefront of attention. This is reflected in the two main developments of surplus theory in recent years.

First, the concepts and propositions developed have been utilised to attack the logical coherence and relevance of 'demand and supply' theories of profit. Second, there has been an attempt to integrate the surplus approach to profit with other theory, especially a Keynesian theory of effective demand. We shall consider each of these matters in subsequent chapters but it is opportune to make some remarks on the second at this stage.

Sraffa's analysis, unlike that of Ricardo and Marx, moves with 'one degree of freedom'. The rate of profit is not determined until the wage is specified, or alternatively the wage is not determined until the rate of profit is specified. As we have seen, Ricardo and Marx developed theories which determined equilibrium real wages at subsistence. But for both logical and empirical reasons these propositions are no longer appealing. There are also difficulties standing in the way of directly developing a sensible theory of wages appropriate to contemporary conditions. One problem is that wage bargaining in modern capitalist economies determines *money* wages, where money is not a commodity in the normal sense but specialised means of payment which are administratively regulated by state agencies. In these circumstances, *numéraire* wages and real wages are not determined until the price level is determined. For this reason and others, closing the system by developing a theory of wages directly is not an approach which has been widely pursued. Instead, most work has concentrated on developing a theory of profit, and of the rate of profit, in terms of a Keynesian theory of effective demand (see Chapter 19). These variables, once determined in this way, can be utilised then in the surplus framework of analysis to determine the other variables. Sraffa himself suggests that such an approach is the more appropriate one.[1]

The integration of the surplus approach with a theory of effective demand can resolve other issues as well. We have repeatedly noticed the segmented or sequential methodology employed by surplus theorists, and in particular the assumption that sectoral outputs are exogenous. This reflects a view in which output levels are seen to be determined independently of the forces acting on relative prices. This bears more than a family resemblance to Keynesian theory or, more specifically, to certain variants of Keynesian theory. Within 'supply and demand' theories outputs are determined simultaneously with relative prices at market-clearing levels. Keynes concentrated his attack on these theories precisely on this issue. According to Keynes, it is 'effective demand', a concept extraneous to 'supply and demand' theories, which determines outputs. Moreover, he provided an analysis in which effective demand could be interpreted as being determined by forces not systematically related to the determinants of relative prices. We need not examine the coherence of these ideas now, but it is clear that according to this interpretation Keynesian economics provided a theory which dovetails neatly into the surplus approach.

If this is accepted, other matters also fall into place and help to explain how surplus theory has developed in recent years. Within Keynesian economics capital accumulation becomes a central concern, for it is a key variable operating on effective demand. But capital accumulation has always been at the forefront for surplus theorists since it pertains to the utilisation of surplus in a capitalist economy. Furthermore, capital accumulation is obviously associated with increases in productive capacity. Growth theory is therefore a natural extension of Keynesian analysis, just as it is in the surplus approach. Also, in following this line of inquiry, both have made links with other work, notably that of Leontief and von Neumann, which had previously been interpreted solely in terms of a supply and demand perspective. In addition, once effective demand, accumulation and growth are seen as central, more specialised topics take a natural place in the scheme: in particular, public finance, monetary theory and international trade. All are pivotal to an elaboration of how effective demand operates in advanced capitalist economies and to the composition, utilisation and realisation of the surplus.[2]

The theory of effective demand and the theory of surplus therefore appear to go hand in hand. However, there is also a tension arising from different perspectives and methods that operates to pull them apart. In the surplus approach attention has been concentrated upon 'centres of gravity' or equilibria defined by the uniformity principle. In addition, the method of analysis abstracts from agents' subjective motivations and perceptions. Garegnani, for example, writes as follows:

> [If we develop] an analysis where the outcome depends upon expectations the assumptions about which can be varied almost indefinitely . . . then theory becomes barren of definite results.[3]

> [By contrast in 'long-period' analysis] the psychological factors summed up in the 'state of confidence' lose much of their force by comparison with objective factors on which the real profitability of investment is supposed to depend.[4]

The perspective of virtually all types of Keynesianism is, however, to concentrate on subjective expectations and the state of confidence. This in turn questions the rationale for focusing upon 'centres of gravity' as surplus theorists understand them. The degree of uncertainty, expectations and the 'state of confidence' are, in Keynesian theory, subject to volatile change, which may preclude the economy attaining any terminal state, or even coming close to such a state. Theories of effective demand and their implications for the determination of profits are therefore not so obviously compatible with surplus theory in its present state of evolution.

Notes to Chapter 8

1. Sraffa (1960, p. 33).
2. On these developments see, for example, Pasinetti (1977a), Harris (1978), Naslund and Sellstedt (1978), Abraham-Frois and Berrebi (1979), Steedman (1977; 1979a; 1979b) and Nell (1980).
3. Garegnani (1973, p. 365).
4. Garegnani (1979, p. 73).

Part III
PROFIT IN SUPPLY AND DEMAND THEORY

9
Characteristics of Supply and Demand Analysis

Supply and Demand Theory

Economic reasoning in terms of supply and demand existed well before the advent of classical political economy. However, it was only in the latter half of the nineteenth century that these concepts began to be formulated rigorously. The greater precision arose from anchoring supplies and demands on to a theory of individual behaviour. Prior to this, 'supply and demand' ideas were used in a very loose fashion and this was one reason why both Ricardo and Marx were contemptuous of these ideas.

The supply and demand analysis which developed after the middle of the nineteenth century is frequently called 'neo-classical'. It arose in different versions. So far as the theory of profit is concerned, the most important ideas have come from the Walrasian, the Austrian and the capital productivity schools of thought. We consider each of these in the following chapters of Part III. Here we concentrate upon the perspective and method generally characteristic of neoclassical theory. These are very different from those which underlie the surplus approach.

Perspective and Methods

The concept of surplus plays no explicit role in neoclassical theories of profit. Instead, neoclassical theorists have been concerned to study how individual economic agents interact through markets. Prime attention is placed upon how these agents' decisions affect the allocation of resources between alternative activities. It is in terms of such decisions that profit is understood.

The context in which this analysis has been carried out has not been that of capitalism in the sense defined above (pp. 11–12). The focus has been upon economies whose activities are co-ordinated by a price system. Of course, neoclassical theorists have been aware that market economies usually involve wage labour. But this has not been considered to be of prime importance in analysis. Instead, it is the exchange of commodities *per se* which has taken central place. Furthermore, economic agents are not conceptualised in terms of social classes. Instead, they are viewed as atomised individuals who fill two roles, that of consumer and producer. In each role, agents have particular 'tastes' or objectives which they seek to satisfy by rational means. As consumers, agents choose consumption goods which are most preferred within the constraint of their limited budgets. A consumer's budget is defined by the assets owned and the prevailing market prices. These assets include labour services and ownership rights in firms, which provide an entitlement to a share in profits. Each consumer's initial endowment of assets is assumed to be exogenous. As producers, agents choose input—output combinations specified by technology which maximises the difference between revenues and costs, i.e. profits. In other words, producers maximise profits subject to a technological constraint. Usually all choices are assumed to be selfish and involve neither malevolence or benevolence towards other agents.

The consumption *plans* of consumers and the production *plans* of producers are supplies and demands. The plan of a consumer involves 'demands' for consumption goods and 'supplies' of factors. The plan of a producer involves 'demands' for factors and 'supplies' of goods. All action, therefore, is specified in terms of demands and supplies, and neoclassical theorists seek to determine *all* endogenous variables, including profits, in terms of the interaction of such supplies and demands.

A balance of supplies and demands or, equivalently, a consistency of agents' plans defines the neoclassical conception of equilibrium. And neoclassical theorists have concentrated attention on equilibria for the same reason as surplus theorists. Equilibria are seen as terminal states. If agents' plans are not mutually consistent, then not all plans can be realised simultaneously. Consequently, at least some agents will change their supplies and demands. Only when supplies and demands balance can all plans be carried out so there is no further motive to change behaviour on the part of any agent. However, during the twentieth century it was realised increasingly by neoclassical theorists that such an equilibrium of demands and supplies would not necessarily exhibit all three properties of the uniformity principle. More specifically, an equilibrium of demands and supplies may involve the price of the same physically specified commodity changing over time. The price of the commodity as input would be different, then, from its price in outputs during a production period.

Finally, segmented or sequential determination is a principle eschewed by the high theorists of neoclassical economics. They favour the simultaneous determination of all economic variables, on the basis of the exogenous data represented by consumers' preferences, producers' technologies and the institutional structure which includes ownership rights to assets:

> The concept of an equilibrium . . . outlined above is applicable as well to the case of a single variable as to so-called general equilibrium involving thousands of variables. Logically the determination of output of a given firm under pure competition is precisely the same as the simultaneous determination of thousands of prices and quantities. In every case *ceteris paribus* assumptions must be made. The only difference lies in the fact that in the general equilibrium analysis . . . the content of the historical discipline of theoretical economics is practically exhausted. The things which are taken as data for that system happen to be matters which economists have traditionally chosen not to consider as within their province. Among these data may be mentioned tastes, technology, the governmental and institutional framework, and many others.[1]

Neoclassical theorists have not always been successful in constructing theory where the exogenous variables are 'non-economic' in this sense. Nevertheless, this is the ideal, and no explanation would be regarded as fully satisfactory, from a theoretical perspective, if it did not conform to it.

Plan of Part III

With the development of neoclassical economics, Walrasian analysis has become increasingly the dominant strand. The theory of profit inherent in this analysis is outlined in Chapter 10. This is followed by the theories of profit developed by Austrian capital theorists and theorists of capital productivity. These do not necessarily conflict with Walrasian theory but their key concepts do not play any significant role in Walrasian analysis.

All these theories of profit have three important characteristics. First, as noted above, they are all theories of equilibrium profits. Second, they are all theories of profit under competitive conditions. Competition is defined as a situation where each agent acts as a price-taker and where all agents face the same set of prices. In other words, every agent acts upon the belief that individual actions will have no effect on market prices. In addition, the market prices prevailing in any period of time are the same for every agent. The relation of market power to profit is considered in Chapter 13. Third, they are theories of profit assuming that all uncertainties are absent. Each agent therefore acts on the belief that the outcome of any action undertaken is perfectly predictable and known. The effect which uncertainties have for neoclassical profit theory is considered in Chapter 13.

In neoclassical terms these three attributes mean that all profit is 'interest' and the two terms, 'profit' and 'interest', will be used as synonyms throughout Chapters 10, 11 and 12. The term 'interest' therefore refers to profits in a competitive equilibrium involving no uncertainty. Any profits over and above interest are called 'pure profits'. Naturally, they are associated with either disequilibria, market power or uncertainty. We shall consider the most important theories of pure profit in Chapter 13.

In Part IV neoclassical theories are subjected to the criticism levelled at them by theorists from the surplus approach to profits. This forms the subject-matter of Chapter 14. In Chapter 15 the boot is on the other foot, and surplus theories are evaluated from the perspective of neoclassical theory.

Note to Chapter 9

1. Samuelson (1947, p. 8). See also Bliss (1975, pp. 28–9, 32, 71–2, 88, 120).

10
Walrasian Intertemporal Theory: Profit, Tastes and Technology

The Nature of Walrasian Theory

The most fundamental development in neoclassical economics during the last third of the nineteenth century is now widely accepted to have been the general-equilibrium analysis of Walras.[1] Schumpeter's sentiments, for example, are typical:

> Economics is a big omnibus which contains many passengers of incommensurable interests and abilities. However, so far as pure theory is concerned, Walras is in my opinion the greatest of all economists. His system of economic equilibrium . . . is the only work by an economist that will stand comparison with the achievements of theoretical physics.[2]

Since the 1930s the significance of Walras's work has become increasingly recognised and his ideas have been developed by neoclassical theorists of the highest calibre.[3] Moreover, the Walrasian school has increasingly placed emphasis upon the logical rigour by which conclusions are reached and stressed that general-equilibrium analysis provides a framework in which *all* neoclassical economics can be developed. Consequently, Schumpeter referred to Walras's early work as the 'Magna Charta of exact economics';[4] and, as such, the development of Walrasian analysis is the principal achievement of neoclassical economics.

In this chapter Walras's early work will not be the prime topic. Instead, concentration is on the major improvements which have been made subsequently and which have culminated in the work of Debreu (1959), and Arrow and Hahn (1971).

The Problems considered by Walrasian Analysis and the Theory of Profit

In a competitive 'free market' economy, composed of self-seeking independent agents, economic activities are related to one another through a system of prices. There is no administrative structure which ensures that the actions of individual agents are co-ordinated. There is only administration of a legal system which enforces contracts voluntarily enacted in markets. Consequently, if 'too much' of some commodity is available, or 'not enough' of another is produced, the only way requisite proportions can be restored is by a change in prices which now encourages agents to reallocate resources in appropriate ways. Intuitively one might expect such a system to function badly, to result in poor co-ordination. Modern Walrasian theory provides formal results which may be used to lend weight to this intuition. However, economists have also been impressed by the fact that 'economic order' can emerge in such an economy. An equilibrium of demands and supplies, in which all agents' plans are consistent, does appear sometimes to occur, at least approximately. Therefore, an important topic of investigation in Walrasian theory has been the question of what conditions will suffice to ensure that such an equilibrium is possible. This has become known as the 'existence' problem. Since detailed empirical knowledge of consumers' tastes, producers' technologies and distributions of assets is not available, and in any case would be of limited usefulness because these things can change, the analysis of 'existence' has tried to formulate propositions in very abstract and therefore general terms. No attempt will be made here to summarise rigorously the results developed.[5] Instead, only an illustration is given. This is all that is required to gain an understanding of neoclassical theories of profit.

We may define the existence problem more precisely as determining whether there is a set of prices, one for each commodity, such that if agents were to maximise on the basis of these prices, the total demands and supplies for each commodity would be such that all agents could realise their plans. This does not require that supplies and demands be equal on each market. The definition allows for a situation where a commodity is so abundant that at no positive price will demand be equal to supply. If such a commodity can be disposed of without cost, then its equilibrium price will be zero and it may be in excess supply. This excess supply poses no problems, however. It does not imply that some agents are not fulfilling their plans. The commodity is free and can be utilised in desired quantities by any agent. Quantities which are superfluous can be freely disposed of. Just as in the case where demand is equal to supply, the market is 'cleared'.

There are a number of conditions which are essential to guarantee the possibility of such an equilibrium. One is that the demands and supplies for each commodity must vary continuously as prices change. Without this property there may be 'gaps in which an inequality between supply and demand can be fitted'.[6] For example, imagine that there are only two types of producer for a particular commodity. One type is 'efficient' and the other is 'inefficient'. For relatively low prices only the 'efficient' producers supply the commodity. But if the price rises to a level which allows the 'less efficient' producers to produce profitably, they will all start simultaneous production resulting in a discontinuous supply. If at such a price demand is not sufficient to take up all output, but at any lower price supply is insufficient to meet demand, then the discontinuity precludes equilibrium. In partial-equilibrium terms the situation could be represented as in Figure 10.1. This is just one example illustrating the requirement for continuity. A host of others could be given, and together they provide powerful support for a view which questions whether economies can be co-ordinated solely through a price mechanism. One should note the status of this result however. When there are discontinuities, equilibrium

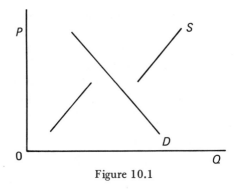

Figure 10.1

cannot be *guaranteed*. It does not mean that equilibrium is impossible. It is important 'not to confuse the statement "an equilibrium cannot be shown to exist" with the statement "no equilibrium is possible" '.[7] Even with pervasive discontinuities, an equilibrium would be possible if they were not operative at equilibrium prices. Equilibrium could occur, but unless discontinuities are ruled out altogether it cannot be guaranteed to be possible.

When we encounter an economy with characteristics consistent with the existence of equilibrium, this does not mean that the economy will always operate in equilibrium. Whether or not the economy is in equilibrium will depend upon the prices which prevail. The existence question is one concerning whether an equilibrium set of prices is possible and not one concerning whether the economy is operating at such a set of prices. Consequently, another question naturally suggests itself. Will the disequilibrium behaviour of the economy tend to establish equilibrium? This is called the 'stability' problem and has also been closely examined by Walrasian economists. The answers given depend upon how agents and markets behave when out of equilibrium; but on the assumptions most commonly employed in this analysis (the Walrasian *tâtonnement* process),[8] the conditions which are required to ensure stability are much more stringent than those required to ensure the existence of equilibrium.[9] Chipman provides a simple example of an unstable equilibrium:

> Suppose there are a great many bakers, each of whom has the same number of infinitely divisible loaves of bread; and

an equal number of churners each of whom has a comparable amount of infinitely divisible butter. Suppose the bakers like to have approximately two slices of bread for each pat of butter, and the churners prefer to have approximately two pats of butter for each slice of bread. Finally let there be initially an equilibrium trade, in which each person keeps two-thirds of his own product and sells the other third.

Now we shall see that this is an unstable equilibrium; that is, the same kind of equilibrium as that of an egg standing on end. Suppose the price of bread is slightly increased. Then the bakers will expect to get more for their bread, so they will have money left over which they will wish to spend on butter; but since bread and butter are complements, if they get more butter they will also want to keep more bread, and sell less than before. Thus the bakers will increase their demand for butter and lower their supply of bread. Similarly, the churners will be penalized by the rise in the price of bread; they will have to buy less, so they will consume less of their own butter and hence supply more.

Now as the bakers are favored by the rise in the price of bread — this is the income effect rightly stressed by Hicks [1939, pp. 67—71] — and the churners disfavored and since the bakers have a relative preference for their own product, it follows that there will be an increase in the excess demand for bread and a fall in the net demand — a rise in the net supply — for butter. Therefore, the price of bread will rise farther still and the price of butter will fall.[10]

If conditions are such as to ensure that an equilibrium exists, this does not necessarily imply that there is only *one* equilibrium. There could be more than one set of prices which would allow all agents to achieve their plans simultaneously. As with the problem of stability, in order to ensure that equilibrium is unique conditions more restrictive than those guaranteeing existence have to be assumed.[11]

An example of non-uniqueness is provided for a two-agent, two-commodity pure exchange economy in the Edgeworth box diagram shown in Figure 10.2. $O_A a_1$ of commodity 1

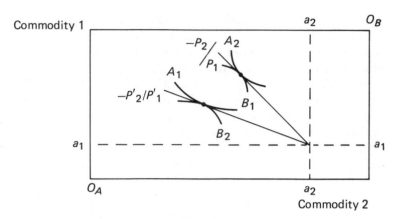

Figure 10.2

and $O_A a_2$ of commodity 2 represent the initial endowment of agent A. $O_B a_1$ of commodity 1 and $O_B a_2$ of commodity 2 constitutes the endowment of agent B. With agents' preferences represented by the indifference curves A_1, A_2, B_1 and B_2 there are two sets of prices, $(p_1 p_2)$ and $(p'_1 p'_2)$, at which supplies and demands for both commodities are equal.

The final problem area considered by Walrasian theorists which we need to mention is that of comparative statics. This is concerned with determining the effect which specified changes in the exogenous data (preferences, technology and the distribution of assets) will have on the equilibrium values of the endogenous variables (prices and quantities traded).

Most neoclassical theories of profit, not just the Walrasian version, have concentrated attention upon profits in equilibrium. They have sought to show the determinants of equilibrium profits, the relation between these profits and the equilibrium values of other variables, and how these profits change as exogenous data changes. Consequently, the analysis of each of the four problems outlined above, that of existence, stability, uniqueness and comparative statics, is of importance to neoclassical theories of profit. An existence proof establishes the logical consistency of a profit theory structured in terms of an equilibrium of demands and supplies. Providing economic processes converge to equilibria, comparative-static propositions allow predictions of how endogenous variables, including profits, will ultimately change as exogenous data are varied. The analysis of uniqueness is of importance for assessing the causal import of neoclassical theory. A theory which seeks to determine the endogenous variables of equilibrium will not be fully deterministic unless equilibrium is unique. Uniqueness is also crucial for comparative statics. If it is to be possible to make clear-cut statements about the equilibrium effects produced by changes in exogenous elements, the analyst must know which equilibria to compare. Without uniqueness this is problematic. Stability analysis indicates the likelihood that equilibria will be established. In doing so, it indicates the weight we may allow propositions about equilibrium patterns to bear. Stability analysis is also important for the method of comparative statics. If equilibria are not stable, quantities and prices which define profits will not converge on those values predicted on the basis of comparisons.

Profits in Intertemporal Equilibrium

A Walrasian equilibrium is open to a number of interpretations. These depend upon the definition of 'commodity' which is used and in terms of which demands, supplies and prices are in turn defined.[12] Obviously, an important distinguishing characteristic of commodities is intrinsic physical characteristics. Ice-cream is clearly not the same commodity as steel. Another distinguishing characteristic, and one which is not so obvious, is the date at which the commodity becomes available. Agents regard 'date of availability' or 'date of delivery' as important. Producers require inputs at specific dates prior to output dates. Consumers' tastes are sensitive to variables related to time, like age. Consequently, it becomes sensible to regard the units of the same physically specified commodity *as different commodities depending upon their date of delivery*. Ice-cream (steel) is not the same commodity 'this week' as ice-cream (steel) 'next week'.

In an economy characterised by *no uncertainty whatever*, producers would know the technology available at every date and consumers would know their tastes and assets at every date. Therefore, agents' plans would cover all dates. Producers would each choose that intertemporal production plan, consistent with technology available at various dates, that would maximise profits calculated over the whole plan. Consumers would each choose an intertemporal consumption plan that they 'most preferred' subject to an intertemporal budget constraint. This budget constraint would state that the total value of demands *over all dates* would have to be no greater than the total value of assets, including labour services, owned *over all dates*. Since the budget is operative as a constraint over all dates *taken together*, this implies that consumers can borrow and lend as they desire and will do so depending upon the intertemporal structure of their tastes and assets. Similarly, producers can, and will, do the same, depending upon the intertemporal structure of their production activities. On these assumptions there would be demands, supplies and markets for every commodity. Markets involving commodities whose date of delivery lay in the future would be 'futures markets', in contrast to 'spot markets' trading in commodities currently available.

The Walrasian definition of equilibrium involves the clearing of *all* markets. This implies that when commodities are defined inclusive of their date of availability, equilibrium involves a balance of supplies and demands on *all* spot and *all* futures markets simultaneously. This further implies that all agents trade in commodities *at one date in time* and that the resulting prices are present-value prices. They are prices which have to be paid in the present, irrespective of the date at which commodities are delivered. Thus the price of steel available fifty-two weeks hence would be a price paid 'this week' for steel to be delivered in one year's time. Such an equilibrium is called an 'intertemporal equilibrium'. The concept was first formulated by Hicks (1939) but has been most developed by Arrow and Debreu.

It is useful to pause for a moment and consider the applicability of this construction. From casual observation it is obvious that a complete set of futures markets does not exist in any market economy. There are some futures markets but they are not comprehensive. Why then bother with such an artificial construction as 'intertemporal equilibrium'? There are two reasons. First, there are some neoclassical economists who would maintain that, even though futures markets are actually incomplete, nevertheless a market economy tends to an equilibrium whose properties are the same, or approximately the same, as those of an intertemporal equilibrium. This implies that the theory of profit implicit in the notion of intertemporal equilibrium is highly relevant to actual market economies. Second, there are other neoclassical economists who maintain that, although actual market economies are unlikely to approach a state resembling an intertemporal equilibrium, nevertheless examining the properties of such an equilibrium allows an understanding of actual market economies. This second view utilises the notion of intertemporal equilibrium as part of a counterfactual methodology. This procedure maintains that one way of understanding the economic importance of, for example, uncertainty is to construct a model in which uncertainty is absent and then compare its results with those results which flow from models incorporating various types of uncertainty. This methodology provides clues to the role which uncertainty has in actual market economies, including the importance of uncertainty upon profits.

On either view, it is important to examine the properties of intertemporal equilibrium. Let us do so in a simple case involving three time periods and three physically distinct commodities. There will be, therefore, nine dated commodities and nine present-value prices that clear the nine markets. Assume that these prices take the numerical values represented in Table 10.1, where date 1 indicates the 'present', i.e. the trading date. Table 10.1 also implies that commodity 1 at

Table 10.1

Physical commodities	Dates		
	1	2	3
1	1	.8	.6
2	4	2	4
3	8	14	20

date 1 acts as *numéraire* but any of the other eight commodities could be utilised for this purpose if desired. If, together with Table 10.1, we also had a list of the quantities traded by each agent and data on the initial ownership of assets, this would completely describe the intertemporal equilibrium.

The profits in such an equilibrium can be determined as follows. It is usual to define the 'own rate of interest' of a physically defined commodity, j, where in Table 10.1 $j = 1$, ..., 3, between two dates, t and $t + \alpha$, where α is an integer lying between 1 and 2, as

$$i_{t, t+\alpha}^{j} = \frac{p_{jt} - p_{j, t+\alpha}}{p_{j, t+\alpha}}$$

The magnitude of this own rate, $i_{t, t+\alpha}^{j}$, indicates the extra amount of good j which can be gained by an agent at $t + \alpha$ for every unit of good j given up at date t. Thus, if an agent reduces demand for commodity 1 at date 1 by one unit he could increase his demand for commodity 1 at date 2 by $1\frac{1}{4}$ units. Consequently he could 'lend' a unit of commodity 1 at date 1 for one period and receive 'interest' of $\frac{1}{4}$ of a unit of commodity 1 from the borrower at date 2. The interest rate applicable to such a loan is $\frac{1}{4}$, or 25 per cent.

The prices in Table 10.1 yield the array of own rates shown in Table 10.2. These rates specify all rates of interest applicable in such an economy. They have three attributes which it is important to notice. They change depending upon the dates over which they relate, they vary between the same two dates depending upon the commodity considered, and some rates are negative.

The change between dates considered is relatively easy to accept because one is used to interest rates in actual economies

Table 10.2

$i_{1,2}^{1} = \frac{1}{4}$	$i_{1,3}^{1} = \frac{2}{3}$	$i_{2,3}^{1} = \frac{1}{3}$
$i_{1,2}^{2} = 1$	$i_{1,3}^{2} = 0$	$i_{2,3}^{2} = -\frac{1}{2}$
$i_{1,2}^{3} = -\frac{3}{7}$	$i_{1,3}^{3} = -\frac{7}{10}$	$i_{2,3}^{3} = -\frac{3}{10}$

changing over time. Variation between goods is a little more difficult to fathom. It arises because the relative prices of the physically specified commodities, at any particular date, vary. If the relative prices p_1/p_2, p_1/p_3, p_2/p_3, were the same at each date, then own interest rates would be the same between any two dates, irrespective of the commodity considered. Relative prices do change of course in actual economies over time, and therefore so too would the commodity own rates of interest between the same two dates. In the intertemporal equilibrium this does not mean agents can gain by lending commodities with the highest own rate of interest. For example, take an agent who is willing to lend one unit of commodity 1 for one period at date 1. If he trades in commodity 1, he receives an own rate of 25 per cent and interest of one-quarter of a unit of commodity 1. If he trades in commodity 2, he would be able to purchase one-quarter of a unit of commodity 2 at date 1, lend it at an own rate of 100 per cent, and receive one-half of a unit of commodity 2 at date 2. But one-half of a unit of commodity 2 at date 2 represents only one unit of purchasing power which translates into one and one-quarter units of commodity 1. This is exactly the same return as achieved by trading in commodity 1. Nor would any loss be sustained if the agent traded in good 3 even though this has a negative own rate of $\frac{3}{7}$. Negative own rates of interest do appear, however, peculiar in their own right. This is because one is used to thinking of (own) *money* rates of interest, where 'money' is a specialised means of exchange with no intrinsic worth, which is never associated with a negative interest rate. There would be no place for 'money' in this sense in an intertemporal equilibrium, for there is no reason why any agent would use it. Here commodities buy commodities directly, and any commodity whose present value rises between two dates will have a negative own rate of interest between these two dates.

We shall say more about the above issues in the next section. But whatever the price structure of an intertemporal equilibrium, once it is specified, together with the set of intertemporal trades between agents, all interest payments and receipts will be determined. Interest receipts represent payments to lenders on *safe* loans by borrowers. They are safe because no element of uncertainty is present. There will be no profits above interest. Pure profits are zero. The reason for this lies in the assumptions of competition, maximising behaviour and no uncertainty. Any activity which allowed of pure profits would be known to all agents. Such activities would then attract resources until prices changed in such a way as to eradicate these gains. Since an equilibrium is a terminal state, no such activities leading to pure profits would exist in equilibrium.[13] This illustrates the counterfactual relevance of the concept of intertemporal equilibrium. If pure profits are other than zero in a context where agents maximise, these profits must be due to disequilibrium, market power or uncertainty. As we shall see in Chapter 13, these are precisely the elements which underlie neoclassical theories of pure profit. The theory of intertemporal equilibrium indicates that these theories are concentrating on elements that lead in the right direction, or, as Schumpeter stated, Walras zero pure profit theorem lies behind 'all clear thinking on profits'.[14]

The Causal Structure lying behind Intertemporal Equilibrium

There is a clear continuity between Walras (1874) and modern formulations of general equilibrium like that of Debreu (1959). The classification of elements into exogenous and endogenous remains the same. Consumers' preferences, technology and the initial distribution of asset ownership together determine the endogenous variables, prices (in terms of which interest rates are defined) and quantities traded. Consequently, if Table 10.2 represents the interest rates of an intertemporal equilibrium, the determinants of these interest rates lie in tastes, technology and asset distribution. If we accept that asset distribution has its effects via consumers' tastes, we can be more succinct and say that the causes of interest rates, and their variation, lie in tastes and technology. For example, when an own rate of interest is negative these two forces must be operating to push up the relevant present-value price over time. One can think of reasons why this could occur. A shift of tastes in favour of a commodity over time and/or increasing difficulty of production over time, coupled with limited or costly storage possibilities, would do this. This example also indicates why the own interest rates of 'money' in an actual modern economy are unlikely ever to be negative. However, as was stated earlier (p. 88), no 'money' exists in the model of intertemporal equilibrium and there are only commodity rates of interest. Furthermore, tastes and technologies which are date-sensitive can easily operate to produce variations in the relative prices of physical commodities over time. These variations lead to different own rates of interest between the same two dates.

Walrasian economists worked their way to this general and abstract conception of the properties of intertemporal equilibrium over a long period of time. Earlier work, some of which was outside the Walrasian tradition, dealt with simpler models and could specify more definite chains of causation. The work of Böhm-Bawerk (1888) and Fisher (1907; 1930) is most relevant in this respect.[15] In order to explain interest, they constructed models in which there was a single dated consumption commodity. The two forces relevant to explaining interest were designated as 'time preference'[16] and the productivity of investment. These forces can in principle operate to generate zero or negative rates of interest, but the emphasis of Böhm-Bawerk and Fisher was upon their role in generating positive interest rates. It was argued that consumers favoured consumption at earlier dates relative to consumption at later dates. Consequently, this time preference acted to raise the present-value price of the consumption good at earlier dates relative to later dates. This implies positive interest rates. In other words, an interest premium had to be paid by borrowers to overcome the time preference in favour of earlier consumption. The productivity of investment reinforced this. A reduction in the consumption of earlier-dated consumption goods would release productive resources which could be employed in investments to increase the outputs of 'later-dated' consumption goods. Moreover, it was assumed that forgone consumption goods could be transformed into a physically larger quantity of later-dated consumption goods. If the present-value prices of a single-dated consumption good were constant, this productivity of investment would allow the receipt of pure profits. Competitive behaviour of profit-maximising producers would operate, therefore, to generate positive interest payments to consumers who would forgo present consumption.

These ideas could be easily utilised to explain profits in a capitalist economy. It is the strength of workers' time preference for present consumption, relative to that of capitalists', which ensures that interest accrues to the latter. Capitalists can 'advance' consumption goods to workers in the form of wages, engage them in productive investment activity, and thereby receive a premium on advances made, i.e. interest. However, Böhm-Bawerk in particular stressed that time preference and investment productivity were universal forces operating in all types of economy.

Böhm-Bawerk did not limit his analysis of profit to the matters discussed above. He also focused considerable attention upon the nature of investment productivity. Together with Jevons (1871) he created what has subsequently become known as the 'Austrian theory of capital', in which the rate of profit is shown to be intimately connected with the intertemporal structure of the inputs required in production. We deal with this aspect of his work in the next chapter.

Notes to Chapter 10

1. Walras (1874).
2. Schumpeter (1954, p. 827).
3. Modern classics of the Walrasian tradition include Hicks (1939), Samuelson (1947), Debreu (1959), and Arrow and Hahn (1971).
4. Schumpeter (1954, p. 568).
5. For such a treatment see Arrow and Hahn (1971).
6. Arrow and Hahn (1971, p. 169).
7. Arrow and Hahn (1971, p. 25).
8. See Arrow and Hahn (1971, pp. 264–70) and this book, pp. 122–4).
9. See Scarf (1960), Negishi (1962), Arrow and Hahn (1971).
10. Chipman (1965, pp. 355–6).
11. See Arrow and Hahn (1971).
12. Debreu (1959, p. x).
13. In the case where producers face diminishing returns, Walrasian theorists sometimes call the economic rents which result *pure profits*. See, for example, Arrow (1971a, p. 70), and Arrow and Hahn (1971, pp. 52–9). This nomenclature is not followed here.

14. Schumpeter (1954, p. 893).
15. On the relation of Fisher's work to that of modern general equilibrium see Samuelson (1967), Hirshleifer (1970), Dougherty (1972; 1980).
16. This is really no more than a reformulation of Senior's concept of 'abstinence'. See Senior (1836). Marshall (1890) preferred the term 'waiting'. Böhm-Bawerk's 'three grounds' for such time preference have been severely criticised. See, for example, Blaug (1978, pp. 527–34), Rogin (1956, ch. 14), Kuenne (1971, pp. 25–43) and Stigler (1941, pp. 25–43). However, the general thrust of Böhm-Bawerk's ideas has been extremely influential, especially through the work of Fisher.

11
Austrian Capital Theory: Profit and 'Roundabout' Production

The Nature of Capital Goods

Böhm-Bawerk (1888) devoted much effort to conceptualising the 'essence' of capital. He believed that Walrasian theory failed fully to incorporate this. The typical Walrasian treatment of 'capital' is in terms of 'capital goods', i.e. physically specified produced means of production. Böhm-Bawerk considered this to be a superficial view. He sought to go 'behind' capital goods and reduce them to *dated* components of labour and land inputs. These latter two factors were regarded as 'original' or 'non-produced' inputs that are ultimately responsible for all production.[1] All produced goods, including capital goods, could therefore, be decomposed into streams of 'dated', 'original' factors.

Böhm-Bawerk considered this conceptualisation to be economically important. Only by working in such a framework could a full appreciation of 'capitalistic production' be accomplished. In particular, only on such a basis could the relationships between commodity values, the capital intensity of the economy, profit and the time structure of production be understood.

It is this emphasis upon the time structure of production which is the defining characteristic of 'Austrian' capital theory. It leads to the classification of Jevons (1871), Wicksell (1901) and Hayek (1931; 1939; 1941) as 'Austrians' because of their similar emphasis. It is also this aspect which Hicks has drawn attention to in labelling his current approach to capital theory as 'neo-Austrian'.[2] In short, the 'Austrian view' is that all economic decisions and processes have a temporal dimension from which it is inappropriate to abstract. The Walrasian notion of intertemporal equilibrium, as outlined in the previous chapter, while incorporating this to some extent does not do so comprehensively. In particular, it does not emphasise the link between capital goods and quantities of dated, original inputs by which they can be produced, i.e. it does not fully come to terms with the intertemporal structure of capitalistic production processes.[3]

Production and Time

Böhm-Bawerk states the Austrian position as follows:

> We put forth our labour in all kinds of wise combinations with natural processes. Thus all that we get in production is the result of two, and only two, elementary productive powers — Nature and Labour . . . There is no place for a third primary resource. [But through] these primary productive powers man may make the consumption goods he desires, either immediately, or through the medium of intermediate products called capital. The latter method demands a sacrifice of time, but it has the advantage in the quantity of the product, and this advantage, although perhaps in decreasing ratio, is associated with every prolongation of the roundabout way of production.[4]

Thus in the Austrian view there are two types of 'original' productive power, labour and land. In fact, Böhm-Bawerk simplified his analysis by abstracting from land and regarding labour as homogeneous. Other Austrians have often followed this lead. Capital goods are goods produced with the aid of original factors and are used as intermediate inputs in the production of consumer goods. Capitalistic production is therefore *indirect* or 'roundabout' production. It is undertaken because it is more productive of consumption goods than is direct production.

In order to isolate the intertemporal nature of capitalistic production, Austrian economists have tended to work with specific types of models. They have been prone to use one-sector models in which there is a single final output, conceived as an aggregate value magnitude or as a homogeneous consumption commodity, but in which there exist many production processes by which the output can be produced. Each such process involves a sequence of 'original' factor inputs applied at various dates. They may be divided into four general types.

(1) The most general is the flow input–flow output process. Original factors are applied at various dates and produce outputs which also occur at various dates. Assuming that such a process operates over n periods it can be represented as:

$$f_n + f_{n-1} + f_{n-2} + \ldots + f_1 \rightarrow b_{n-1} + b_{n-2} + \ldots + b_0$$

$$(11.1)$$

Period 0 may be taken to be the 'present' and the subscript n would then indicate 'n periods' before the present; $f_i(i = 1, \ldots, n)$ represent the inputs of labour at time i; and $b_i(i = 0, \ldots, n - 1)$ the outputs of the consumption good at date i. Some f_i and b_i may be zero. This representation does not imply that capital goods are absent from production, it is just that capital goods are not explicitly shown. For example, f_n may produce an intermediate output as well as b_{n-1}. The other $f_i(i = 1, \ldots, n - 1)$ utilise this intermediate capital good to produce outputs of the consumption goods at other dates. It is also important to stress that the f_i and b_i are not 'historical' quantities in 'real' time. The series of labour inputs and outputs are series derived from the current technology (see pp. 132–5). Or, in the Austrian view, the relationship between f_i and b_i *is* the proper representation of the current technology.

(2) A specialisation of the above is the point input–flow output process. Here there is no flow of original factor inputs. Instead, they are applied at one date only, though outputs occur at various points in time.

(3) An alternative specialisation is the flow input—point output type of process. Inputs occur at various dates but output results only at a single date.

(4) The most restrictive special case is to combine the special attributes of (2) and (3) into a point input—point output process.

The earliest Austrian capital theorists, Jevons, Böhm-Bawerk and Wicksell, concentrated their analysis on the latter two types. They were, however, aware of the general framework and did attempt some conceptualisation of the other types of processes, believing that their approach could encompass them all.[5] Nevertheless, this concentration of analysis on types (3) and (4) meant that fixed capital was excluded from the formal analysis. Fixed capital, within the single-sector framework, implies that inputs yield outputs at more than one point in time. It is not durability, *per se*, that is analytically relevant. It is that fixed capital necessarily leads to intertemporal joint production, the production of the final output at various points in time resulting from one set of inputs.

'Roundaboutness', Equilibrium and Profit

It is in terms of this time-based framework that Austrian capital and profit theory works. The theorists sought to show the relationship between time structure and valuation, between time structure and capital intensity, and between time structure and distribution.

Technically efficient production processes are ordered by their degree of roundaboutness. The more roundabout production processes are more productive of consumption goods per unit of original factor input, but are subject to diminishing returns. An increase in roundaboutness relative to the inputs of original factors increases final output, but such increments to increasing roundaboutness decrease.[6] Pivotal to this conception is a definition of the degree of roundaboutness. Böhm-Bawerk's principal measure is the 'average period of production'.[7] Assuming production takes place over n periods, any production process of the flow input—point output type can be represented as follows:

$$f_n + f_{n-1} + f_{n-2} + \ldots + f_1 \to b_0 \tag{11.2}$$

f_i is the input of labour i periods prior to when final output accrues $(i = 1, \ldots, n)$; b_0 represents one unit of final output. The average period of production of such a process is defined as:

$$T = \frac{\sum\limits_{i=1}^{n} f_i i}{\sum\limits_{i=1}^{n} f_i} \tag{11.3}$$

(This formula also applies to processes of the point input–point output type. In this case the average period is equal to the absolute period, n.) The numerator represents the sum of the original factor inputs weighted by the time in which they remain in production. The denominator is the unweighted sum of these factor inputs. Therefore, T expresses the 'average' period that labour inputs are required in the production process before the emergence of final output.

Böhm-Bawerk maintains that roundaboutness and capital intensity are directly related.[8] He therefore uses T both as a measure of roundaboutness and of capital intensity. To do so, however, implies that profit accrues on the basis of simple interest, not compound interest (see below, pp. 99–101). If profit is calculated on the basis of simple interest, then T is equal to the capital–labour ratio when capital is measured in wage units or 'command over labour'. The equilibrium value of output associated with the process when operated under competition is equal to its cost of production including profit. This cost of production is equal to

$$\sum_{i=1}^{n} w f_i (1 + ir) \tag{11.4}$$

where w is the wage rate and r is the rate of profit. The wage bill is equal to

$$\sum_{i=1}^{n} w f_i \tag{11.5}$$

Total profits are therefore equal to

$$\sum_{i=1}^{n} wf_i(1 + ir) - \sum_{i=1}^{n} wf_i = rw \sum_{i=1}^{n} f_i i \qquad (11.6)$$

If K represents the value of capital on which profits are paid at the rate of r, then profits equal rK. Consequently

$$K = w \sum_{i=1}^{n} f_i i \qquad (11.7)$$

Dividing (11.7) through by (11.5) we have

$$K^* \Bigg/ \sum_{i=1}^{n} f_i = \sum_{i=1}^{n} f_i i \Bigg/ \sum_{i=1}^{n} f_i = T \qquad (11.8)$$

where K^* is measured in wage units.

The Austrian conceptualisation of production could be integrated into Walrasian theory without any difficulty. There is nothing in the Austrian conception of dated 'original' factors producing final outputs which precludes such a treatment. (However, see pp. 132—5.) Böhm-Bawerk, nevertheless, did not adopt this approach. He disliked the Walrasian framework for many reasons[9] and chose instead a non-Walrasian formulation which concentrates upon the production sector of the economy. He assumed that the following conditions apply:[10]

1. There exist a number of technically efficient productive processes each of a different degree of roundaboutness. Each can produce final outputs and can be represented as a set of dated labour inputs prior to output.
2. There are diminishing returns to increasing roundaboutness.
3. There is a given labour force made up of homogeneous 'labourers'.
4. Competition and maximising behaviour prevail, though profit is assumed to accrue on a simple interest basis.
5. There is a fixed wage fund or amount of capital measured in value terms. (Böhm-Bawerk uses the terms 'subsistence fund' and 'capital' as interchangeable.)[11] Final output is also measured in value terms.[12]

The equilibrium wage and rate of profit are determined by two conditions: first, the condition that the supply of labour be equal to the demand for labour; second, the processes in which labour is employed are assumed to maximise profits. The rate of profit in such an equilibrium is related to the 'marginal product of roundaboutness': 'The rate of interest . . . is limited and determined by the productiveness of the last extension of the process economically permissible.'[13]

This equilibrium is most appropriately seen as a stationary state in which the economy simply reproduces itself in every time period, without a change in scale and where the uniformity principle applies. Böhm-Bawerk utilises the comparison of different such equilibria to deduce effects which capital accumulation will have on the rate of profit, assuming technology remains unchanged:

> In a community [the rate of] interest will be high in proportion as the national subsistence fund is low, as the number of labourers employed by the same is great, and as the surplus returns connected with any further expansion of the production period continue high. Conversely [the rate of] interest will be low the greater the subsistence fund, the fewer the labourers and the quicker the fall in surplus returns.[14]

This also implies that the wage rate is inversely related to the rate of interest. Consequently, as the rate of profit declined the wage rate would rise.

Austrian Capital Theory and Neoclassical Economics

The determination of the wage and rate of profit in the model outlined on pages 96–9 is flawed in a number of respects. One of these relates to the properties Böhm-Bawerk incorporated into his measure of roundaboutness, i.e. the average period of production. As we have already noted (p. 97), he considered the average period of production to be an index of time structure and an index of capital intensity. However, this is only valid if profit accrues on the basis of simple interest, which contradicts the assumption of maximising behaviour. Wicksell realised this. The equilibrium value of output in expression (11.2) is equal to

$$\sum_{i=1}^{n} wf_i(1+r)^i \qquad (11.9)$$

The wage bill is given by (11.5) as

$$\sum_{i=1}^{n} wf_i \qquad (11.5)$$

Total profits are therefore equal to

$$\sum_{i=1}^{n} wf_i(1+r)^i - \sum_{i=1}^{n} wf_i \qquad (11.10)$$

The value of the capital stock is

$$\frac{1}{r} \sum_{i=1}^{n} wf_i(1+r)^i - \sum_{i=1}^{n} wf_i \qquad (11.11)$$

Dividing (11.11) by (11.5) gives the capital–labour ratio, with capital measured in wage units, as

$$\frac{\sum_{i=1}^{n} f_i(1+r)^i - \sum_{i=1}^{n} f_i}{r \sum_{i=1}^{n} f_i} \qquad (11.12)$$

This is not equal to T as given by equation (11.3). Expression (11.12) is a function of the rate of profit, while (11.3) is independent of the rate of profit.

Nevertheless, the significance of this defect is not great. Capital intensity and roundaboutness are analytically separate concepts. Capital intensity is an index of the ratio of produced means of production to original factors, while roundaboutness is an index of the time structure of production. Wicksell certainly did not see the defect in Böhm-Bawerk's reasoning on the average period of production as central. He accepted the conceptualisation of production structure in terms of time and built his capital theory upon it.

Most subsequent neoclassical economists have not done so. The reason for this was not that they found compelling defects in the basic message of Austrian theory, though there were criticisms of the Austrians' own treatment.[15] Rather, it was because the message was difficult to translate into definite implications. One could accept that Böhm-Bawerk had established the temporal properties of capital goods and yet still wonder of what use these properties could be put to in developing theory. Hayek (1931; 1939; 1941) had tried to establish the usefulness of the Austrian vision but his work was not only unclear, it was also against the Keynesian spirit of the times. The recent work of Hicks (1970; 1973a; 1973b; 1975; 1976), which is far superior to that of other Austrians, has also not convinced most neoclassical economists that the Austrian conception has advantages over that of the Walrasian.[16] The scepticism of Clark (1894; 1895) proved particularly influential. Clark, followed by Knight (1933), argued that, in a stationary state, production was synchronised with consumption, so that the explicit consideration of time structure was redundant. Current consumption could be viewed *as if* it were a function of current inputs.[17] Furthermore, the distributional relationships which the Austrians had sought to establish could be explained more easily through the use of synchronised models. In the next chapter we consider Clark's theory, which traces profit directly to the productivity of capital.

Notes to Chapter 11

1. See Gaitskell (1936; 1938).
2. Hicks (1970; 1973a; 1973b; 1975; 1976).
3. The basic conception of Austrian theory is much older than Böhm-Bawerk. See Schumpeter (1954, pp. 465, 469, 564–7, 594, 636–7, 846, 902–3).
4. Böhm-Bawerk (1888, p. 91). See also Wicksell (1893, pp. 20–1; 1901, pp. 150, 154; 1900, p. 108; and 1911, p. 185).
5. See, for example, Böhm-Bawerk (1888, bk VI, chs 7, 8) and Jevons (1871, pp. 231, 238–9).

6. Böhm-Bawerk (1888, pp. 20, 84–5, 91, 99, 260–2, 269–70, 355). See also Jevons (1871, pp. 240–1).

7. See, for example, Gaitskell (1936; 1938).

8. Böhm-Bawerk (1888, p. 325), Jevons (1871, pp. 229–31). See also Stigler (1941, pp. 201–4).

9. See, for example, Schumpeter (1952, pp. 143–90; and 1954, pt IV).

10. Böhm-Bawerk (1888, bk VII, chs 2–5).

11. See, for example, Böhm-Bawerk (1888, pp. 401–2).

12. See also Schumpeter (1954, p. 998).

13. Böhm-Bawerk (1888, pp. 393–4). See also Jevons (1871, pp. 240–1).

14. See Böhm-Bawerk (1888, p. 401). Jevons drew the same conclusions – see Jevons (1871, p. 245) – as did Wicksell (1901, p. 209).

15. See, for example, Fisher (1907), Knight (1933), Kaldor (1937), Gaitskell (1936; 1938), Hicks (1939), Stigler (1941), Schumpeter (1954) and Blaug (1978).

16. See Burmeister (1974).

17. On this matter see also Schumpeter (1954, pp. 564–5, 907), Blaug (1978, pp. 196, 549), Stigler (1941, pp. 296, 313), and Kaldor (1937, pp. 170–3).

12
The Neoclassical Theory of Capital Productivity: Profit determined by the Supply of and the Demand for Capital

Capital Productivity

The defining quality of this group of neoclassical theorists is the treatment of 'capital' as a factor of production formally equivalent to other factors like land and labour. It was believed that factor prices vary inversely with relative scarcities and are determined by supply and demand. Consequently, the rate of profit, conceived as the price of capital within this approach, is determined by the supply and demand for capital and declines as capital becomes less scarce.

The major theorists involved in the development of this analytical framework are Clark (1899),[1] Hicks (1932), Solow (1956), and Samuelson (1962). Its roots lie in a particular interpretation of Ricardo's theory of diminishing returns and rent.[2] Clark considered Ricardo's theory as one in which the composite factor (labour and capital) received a remuneration equal to its marginal product and land received the residual difference between the sum of these payments and total output. Clark generalised this into the principle that *any* variable factor received a remuneration equal to its marginal product and *any* fixed factor received the remainder. Thus, since in theory each factor may be considered variable or fixed, the principle of marginal productivity is of universal application.[3] In equilibrium all factors will receive a return based upon their marginal productivities. Given diminishing returns to the employment of any variable factor[4] and the equality, in equilibrium, of the marginal product of capital with the rate of profit,[5] it follows that as capital becomes relatively less scarce, the rate of profit declines and other factor prices, including the wage, rise.[6]

A requirement for this set of propositions to form an internally coherent whole is that the distributional relations based upon marginal productivity be consistent with the technological relations between inputs and outputs. This implies that the total product be equal to the sum of factor payments when each factor is paid according to its marginal productivity. Wicksteed (1894) and Flux (1894) provided a solution to this problem. They proved that if the production function exhibited constant returns to scale, then the payment of factors according to their marginal productivities would exactly exhaust output.[7]

Prior to Hicks (1932) marginal productivity theory was a theory of input prices. Hicks sought to deal with factor shares and formalised those properties of the production function relevant to this problem in the concept of the elasticity of substitution.[8] This was used in relation to an aggregate production function, the arguments of which consisted of aggregate capital and labour. Hicks also sought to analyse the distributional effects resulting from a shift in such a production function. In doing so he introduced his famous classification of technical change.[9] With these analytic developments Hicks added to Clark's earlier formulation a theory of relative shares in income which involved three determinants: relative input quantities, the elasticity of substitution and the direction of bias in technical change.

Clark and Hicks were both explicit in confining their analysis to stationary states and their comparison where the uniformity principle holds.[10] Thus, although the purpose of both was to analyse a process of capital accumulation, the method was one of comparisons. The rationale for this lay in the belief shared by Böhm-Bawerk: 'A comparison of a sequence of stationary states . . . [would] give a first approximation to a slow process of steady accumulation.'[11]

Growth was introduced into the capital productivity framework by Solow (1956). However, this did not involve a significant break with the stationary framework utilised by previous theorists. Solow assumed that there was only one produced commodity which was perfectly malleable and could be either invested or consumed. The decisions as to how much of the commodity to use as capital in the following period and how much was to be consumed could be made at the end of every production period and did not affect the economic processes operative during that period. Consequently, the growth path could be conceived as one whose form did not differ from a movement through successive stationary states. Furthermore, Solow made other assumptions which ensured a convergence to a steady-state equilibrium. The growth path thereby took the form of a movement between stationary states which differed only by a scale factor.

On the basis of Solow's analysis there developed many further results. Various paths of growth and distributional change could be analysed, each dependent on the assumptions which governed the form of the production function, the type of technical progress, the supply of capital and initial endowments of resources.[12] Also associated with this theoretical work were attempts at empirical testing and application. Starting in 1928, Cobb and Douglas used an aggregate production function to explain time-series and cross-section data drawn from the US economy.[13] The results were interpreted as supporting the theory of capital productivity with distribution determined by marginal productivity. Solow (1957) extended this to locate and measure the sources of growth in the US economy. These studies, however, are only the most notable of a large set.[14]

Capital, the Marginal Product of Capital and the Rate of Profit

Essential to the theoretical structure of the productivity theorists is a precise conceptualisation of capital. Clark dealt with this at length.[15] He made a distinction between capital and capital *goods*. Capital goods are heterogeneous, non-permanent and relatively fixed in areas of utilisation. Capital, on the other hand, is homogeneous, permanent and mobile. It denotes a fund of abstract productive power whose components are capital goods which change over time (land is also included as a component of capital). There is therefore a metaphysical aura that surrounds Clark's discussion of capital. Since the marginal product which determines the rate of profit is the marginal product of 'capital',[16] there is considerable ambiguity as to the exact definition of this marginal product. Clark does, however, frequently measure capital by aggregating capital goods in terms of their values.[17] As we shall see (p. 107), this is the correct procedure, given the results he was attempting to establish.

The same lack of clarity in the definition of capital concepts exists in Hicks (1932). Shove emphasised this in his perceptive review: 'Unfortunately "capital" is not defined and we are not told how quantities of it . . . are to be measured, and similarly with "saving".'[18]

Clark and Hicks are by no means exceptional. It has been a general attribute of those economists of the capital productivity school to be vague as to the exact specification of their concepts of capital.[19] This was pointed out most forcibly by Robinson:

> The production function has been a powerful instrument of miseducation. The student of economic theory is taught to write $O = F(L, C)$ where L is the quantity of labour C a quantity of capital and O a rate of output of commodities. He is instructed to assume all workers are alike and to measure L in man-hours of labour; he is told something about the index number problem involved in choosing a unit of output; and then he is hurried on to the next question, in the hope that he will forget to ask in what units C is measured.[20]

There is, of course, no difficulty in defining capital as distinct from capital goods. Capital goods can be aggregated into 'capital' in many different ways. The problem is not in aggregation *per se* but in doing so in such a way as to yield the results of productivity theory. The procedure must allow the rate of profit to be an inverse function of the scarcity of capital and to bear a relation of equality to its marginal product. This last requirement means capital must be measured in values. Unless capital is defined to be *value* capital it would not be possible for its marginal product to be equal to the rate of profit. The price of a unit of some physical capital's services in equilibrium − its net rental rate − is the rate of profit multiplied by the price of a unit of that capital good. Thus we require the price of a unit of the capital good to be equal to 1.0 for its net rental rate to equal the rate of profit. In other words, the rate of profit is a pure number; it expresses a percentage per unit of time. If a marginal product is to be equal to it, it must be expressible as a pure number. The marginal value product of a unit of physical capital is the (infinitesimal) small addition to the value of net outputs over the (infinitesimal) small addition to the physical capital that this is associated with. It is therefore not a pure number except in special cases. To make it such we have to make a unit of capital a unit of value, i.e. to measure capital goods in terms of their values. We can then talk of a marginal product of *capital* as a pure number and it has a chance of being equal to the rate of profit.

The Determination of the Rate of Profit by the Supply of and the Demand for Capital

The measurement of capital in terms of the values of capital goods undermines the *determination* of the rate of profit by the supply of and the demand for capital. In neoclassical theory supplies and demands represent the plans of optimising agents regarding choices over commodities. It is these supplies and demands, or choices, which determine the endogenous variables. If capital is specified to be value capital, then it does not possess the attribute a commodity *must* possess for determination by supply and demand to be valid. It cannot, except in special cases, be defined independently of endogenous variables. The unit of measurement is dependent on equilibrium prices and these prices are in general endogenous variables. It is therefore not possible to regard economic agents as forming plans (demands and supplies) for capital, the interaction of which then *determines* its price, the rate of profit. The logical structure of determination requires that the determinants be exogenous, and this is impossible in the case of the demand for and supply of capital. This consideration also undermines the logic of Böhm-Bawerk's procedure for determining the rate of profit (which we discussed above, pp. 98—9). Value capital cannot be taken as an exogenous variable in the manner of Böhm-Bawerk or Clark.

This point was clearly perceived by Wicksell at the turn of the century:

> Whereas labour and land are measured each in terms of its own *technical* unit . . . capital, on the other hand . . . is reckoned . . . as a sum of *exchange value* . . . a unit extraneous to itself. However good the practical reasons for this may be, it is a theoretical anomaly which disturbs the correspondence which would otherwise exist between all the factors of production.[21]

Obviously, if the supply of and demand for value capital cannot be considered determinants of the rate of profit, one cannot maintain that the marginal product of an exogenously specified supply of such capital will determine the rate of profit. It is not valid, in general, to regard the supply of capital as an exogenous variable and its marginal product to be a variable defined by technology independent of valuation. At most, this marginal product could only *equal* the rate of profit. Wicksell, also proved that, in general, this equality would not hold.[22] However, Wicksell did believe that the marginal product of capital would always be less than the rate of profit so that there would be an inverse relationship exhibited between the capital intensity of an economy and its rate of profit (see pp. 139—40).

Wicksell's criticisms were repeated, and indeed extended, by others in the twentieth century.[23] Their effect upon the theory of capital productivity was to force its exposition and development into models in which there is a single produced commodity. This commodity was produced by itself and homogeneous labour, so the production sector of the economy could be represented by an aggregate production function whose arguments were labour and capital.[24] In such a model physical capital can be taken to be value capital and it is legitimate to treat the supply of capital as exogenous. Furthermore, the rate of profit will be determined by the supply and demand for capital, and for any predetermined stock of capital the rate of profit will be determined by, and equal to, the marginal product of capital.[25] This model was recognised to be an extreme simplification of any actual economy, but it was argued that the relationships which it exhibited between capital intensity, the wage and rate of profit held generally. In other words, although it could be admitted that, in general, it was invalid to regard the supply of and demand for value capital as determinants of anything, nevertheless the relationships derived by developing a special case in which they could be considered determinants were generally valid relationships. As a consequence, the 'one-commodity model' could be used as a 'parable' to illustrate relationships exhibited by actual economies.[26] It follows, then, that whatever validity exists in the neoclassical theory of capital productivity must be confined to the relationships which it establishes between economic variables: that is, the capital intensity of the economy, the wage and rate of profit. These relationships will be critically examined in Chapter 14.

Notes to Chapter 12

1. The propositions of this approach are much older than the work of Clark. See, for example, Schumpeter (1954, pp. 464–9, 656–7, 1032), Dobb (1973, pp. 96–120) and Meek (1967, pp. 51–74). Clark, however, was the first to provide a systematic exposition of these ideas in the 1880s and 1890s. Since then it has been the convention to regard him as the principal founder of the theory.
2. Schumpeter (1954, pp. 674, 868, 936). See also Hicks (1932, p. 112).
3. Clark (1899, pp. 188–205). Clark was not alone in formulating this generalisation. It was also accomplished by Wicksteed (1910) and Wicksell (1901).
4. Clark (1899, pp. 38, 165, 197–8, 208).
5. Clark (1899, pp. ix–x, 21, 160, 187, 249, 255).

6. Clark (1899, pp. 184—6).
7. See, for example, Stigler (1941, ch. 12) and Johnson (1973, ch. 3).
8. Hicks (1932, pp. 117—20).
9. Hicks (1932, p. 121).
10. Clark (1899, pp. vi, 12, 60, 399—430), Hicks (1932, pp. 6, 113; 1963, pp. 335—6, 338, 342, 345, 366). See also Schumpeter (1954, p. 565).
11. Champernowne (1953, p. 77). See also Schumpeter (1954, pp. 564—5, 868, 929—30, 1022) and Johnson (1973, pp. 129—30).
12. See, for example, Hahn and Matthews (1964) and Johnson (1966).
13. Cobb and Douglas (1928), and Douglas (1948).
14. See, for example, Harcourt (1972).
15. Clark (1899, ch. 9).
16. Clark (1899, pp. ix—x, 21, 160, 187, 249, 255).
17. Clark (1899, pp. 119—21, 157).
18. Shove (1933, p. 264). In his 'Commentary' on *The Theory of Wages* in 1963, Hicks aggregates capital goods through values. See Hicks (1963, p. 344).
19. See, for example, Stigler (1941).
20. Robinson (1953, p. 47).
21. Wicksell (1901, p. 149). See also Wicksell (1900, pp. 107—8).
22. Wicksell (1901, pp. 172—84, 209; 1923, p. 293).
23. See Shove (1933), Lange (1936), Metzler (1950), Malinvaud (1953), Robinson (1953), Champernowne (1953), and Swan (1956).
24. See, for example, Solow (1956), Swan (1956), Meade (1961), Hahn and Matthews (1964), and Johnson (1966).
25. See Howard (1979, pp. 95—101).
26. Samuelson (1962).

13
Pure Profit: Innovation, Uncertainty and Market Power

Zero Pure Profits

The neoclassical theories covered in the preceding three chapters are all theories of *interest*. The profits analysed by these theories are profits in competitive equilibria and assume that uncertainty is of no importance. In such a context no agent will pay or receive a premium above the ruling rate of interest, nor will any agent pay or receive interest at a lower rate. There are zero pure profits. The status of such theories is a controversial issue among neoclassical economists. Disputes arise over a number of matters, including the relevance of the competitive assumption, how likely it is that economies will operate in, or close to, equilibria, and the significance which various types of uncertainty have. However, even if one takes the view that competition is limited, that uncertainty results in very different economic patterns, and that economies are rarely close to equilibria of supplies and demands, the theories of competitive equilibria in a context of certainty are still useful. They provide a benchmark with which to assess the importance of any deviation from the assumptions upon which they rest. Indeed, the principal theorists of pure profit, Schumpeter (1912; 1939) and Knight (1921), both developed their analyses in this way.

Before moving on to consider these theories of pure profit, it will be useful to deal briefly with the notion of a Walrasian temporary equilibrium. This construction was first utilised by Walras[1] but was later refined by Hicks (1939), and it is from Hicks that most subsequent work on temporary equilibrium has sprung. Viewing the theories of Schumpeter and Knight from this perspective of temporary equilibrium throws them into a clearer light.

Walrasian Temporary Equilibrium

In Chapter 10 we outlined the theory of Walrasian inter-temporal equilibrium. This was an equilibrium involving markets for all commodities over all dates. Consequently, there is a single trading date. In actual economies, markets do not exist on such a comprehensive basis and trading is sequential. The notion of temporary equilibrium has been used to take account of this.

Hicks (1939) conceptualises the matter as follows. There are a number of periods, and at the beginning of each spot markets exist together with a limited number of futures markets covering those commodities which can be traded on a forward basis. Since futures markets are not comprehensive, agents have to estimate some future prices in order to carry out optimal current transactions. On the basis of these expectations, agents trade in those commodities for which markets exist. Equilibrium is a situation where there is a consistency of agents' plans involving commodities on these markets, i.e. it involves only a balance of supplies and demands on the operating markets. The contracts which have been made govern agents' behaviour during the rest of the period. At the beginning of the next period markets 're-open' and new trading can occur. Depending upon what has happened in the first period, and upon the state of the markets in the second period, the expectations formed at the beginning of the first period may turn out to be correct or incorrect in varying degree. Therefore, expectations may be revised and market prices in the second period will reflect these new expectations. At the start of the third period, markets re-open again. The economy thus proceeds through a sequence of temporary equilibria.

A temporary equilibrium is therefore an equilibrium on a restricted set of markets and is dependent upon agents' price expectations. Consequently, it is very different from the notion of intertemporal equilibrium dealt with in Chapter 10. However, the problems of existence, stability, uniqueness and comparative statics of intertemporal equilibrium have their counterparts in the temporary equilibrium framework. For example, it can be shown that the conditions required to guarantee the existence of a temporary equilibrium are essentially the same as those which ensure the existence of intertemporal equilibrium. In particular, demands and supplies must vary continuously with market prices. Such matters are not our prime concern but they need to be remembered. They reinforce the point made earlier (pp. 79–84) that all equilibrium theory, including an equilibrium theory of profit, may be of limited applicability.

There are two other general issues which it is advisable to note in relation to temporary equilibrium. First, in terms of a strict interpretation of neoclassical methodology (outlined on pp. 73–6) the model of temporary equilibrium just described is questionable. To *assume* the absence of some markets is really illegitimate. Rather, the number of markets operating should be explained endogenously in terms of agents' behavior. Neoclassical economists sensitive to this have sought to explain the absence of markets in terms of particular forms of uncertainty and transactions costs. The intertemporal model of Chapter 10 assumed agents were fully aware of the commodities available on each date, the technologies which could be used on each date, their assets and their intertemporal tastes. In addition, the cost of any transaction was assumed to be zero. Under these circumstances it is not surprising that *all* markets exist. Furthermore, once these assumptions are relaxed, the fact that some markets may not emerge ceases to be problematic. Agents may be unwilling to trade or there may not be mutually beneficial prices at which trade can take place. These considerations are thought to have their effect, primarily, in inhibiting the development of a comprehensive set of futures markets.[2] They also allow 'real-world' phenomena like money, stock markets and speculation to find a place in the neoclassical scheme.

Second, these matters are relevant beyond the question of
which markets exist. Transactions costs and particular forms
of uncertainty affect the kind of markets which exist. In
particular, they may operate in such a way as to conflict with
the defining quality of competition. For example, in a context
where there is not a full complement of futures markets,
agents' current transactions, which include borrowing and
lending, depend upon their expectations of future prices. An
agent may, therefore, make contracts which subsequent events
show to have been based on faulty expectations. These events
may be such as to increase the difficulty, or altogether preclude, the fulfilling of these contracts. Lenders will know this
and will also know that there may be heavy costs involved in
their attempt to enforce contracts. Consequently, they will
attempt to assess the 'creditworthiness' of borrowers, and the
operation of this can run contrary to the assumption of competition, which implies that agents can freely trade at para-
metric prices. Therefore, once one jettisons the intertemporal
framework, recognition of imperfect competition naturally
suggests itself (see also pp. 122—4).

Temporary and Intertemporal Equilibrium

The prices and trades of any temporary equilibrium depend
upon agents' expectations of the prices which will prevail in
the future. Furthermore, the path of an economy traced out
by a sequence of temporary equilibria depends upon how
correct agents' expectations turn out to be and how any errors
make their effect upon the revision of expectations. However,
such a sequence could conceivably mirror an intertemporal
equilibrium.

Let us assume agents hold their expectations about future
prices, goods available in the future, technologies existing in
the future and future tastes with perfect confidence. Every
agent would then formulate an intertemporal plan, though
the absence of some markets would mean that each agent
could not complete trades at the initial date but would have
to do so sequentially as the relevant markets come into opera-
ation. If agents' expectations turn out to be correct, or, as

some neoclassical economists would say, their expectations are 'rational', this would mean their intertemporal plans were consistent. Each agent's price expectations would be compatible with all markets clearing when these markets come into operation. Provided there exists one futures market in the initial period, which covers all dates, and agents never run into a 'creditworthy' constraint, the sequence of temporary equilibria would exactly mirror that of an intertemporal equilibrium involving a complete set of futures markets, one trading date and zero pure profits.

It is in terms of such a sequence of temporary equilibria that both Schumpeter (1912) and Knight (1921) developed their theories of pure profit. In both cases the purpose was the same: namely, to isolate the causes of non-zero pure profit by constructing a model where pure profits did not exist and then change the assumptions in a particular way, so tracing out the central determinants of pure profit.

Schumpeter: Innovation as the Cause of Pure Profits

In the sequence of temporary equilibria discussed in the previous section, agents forecast market-clearing prices with perfect accuracy. Schumpeter rationalises such a state of affairs by constructing a model where the structure of determinants, i.e. tastes, technology and asset distribution, has been existent long enough for agents to incorporate completely the economic implication of this structure into their forecasting procedures. If agents are rational, any knowledge which improves forecasting ability will have economic value. Schumpeter assumes that the structure has been invariant for a sufficiently long enough time for all relevant knowledge to have been sought out so that accurate forecasts become 'routinised': 'The assumption that conduct is prompt and rational is in all cases a fiction. But it proves to be sufficiently near to reality, if things have time to hammer logic into men.'[3] In such circumstances pure profits will be zero. Schumpeter calls this sequence of temporary equilibria with rational expectations 'the circular flow'. He seems to conceive of it primarily as a stationary state involving a zero rate of interest.[4] However, neither the stationary characteristic nor the proposition that the interest rate is zero is necessary to his theory of pure profit.

In Schumpeter's view what is central is the invariance of structure. This is what explains the accuracy of expectations. Pure profits different from zero are traced, therefore, to changes in this structure. These changes are referred to as 'innovations' and are defined as follows:

> This concept covers the following five cases: (1) The introduction of a new good — that is one with which consumers are not yet familiar — or of a new quality of a good. (2) The introduction of a new method of production, that is one not yet tested by experience in the branch of manufacture concerned, which need by no means be founded upon a discovery scientifically new, and can also exist in a new way of handling a commodity commercially. (3) The opening of a new market, that is a market into which the particular branch of manufacture of the country in question has not previously entered, whether or not this market has existed before. (4) The conquest of a new source of supply of raw materials or half-manufactured goods, again irrespective of whether this source already exists or whether it has first to be created. (5) The carrying out of the new organisation of any industry.[5]

Innovations are conceived to result from the action of entrepreneurs, who are agents with superior imagination, leadership and organisational abilities.[6] The entrepreneurial-engendered innovations change the structure and disrupt the routine. Pure profits arise from the market power inherent in successful innovation. An entrepreneur being 'first in the field' has a monopoly position allowing prices to exceed costs of production.[7]

These pure profits will be temporary because the market power on which they are based is temporary. Once possibilities for positive pure profits are recognised by other agents, the activities of innovating entrepreneurs will be imitated and market power, together with pure profits, will wain. The speed with which this occurs varies depending upon the obstacles which exist for such emulation.[8]

Innovations produce positive pure profits for other sectors of the economy while they are in the process of creation. These are 'windfalls' and depend upon the primary innovating activity.[9] Like this they are inherently temporary because recognition of their existence leads other agents to reallocate resources which undermine them. When the innovation is established its impact undermines the position of other activities and create losses for them. Schumpeter referred to this process as one of 'creative destruction'.[10]

Pure profits can be calculated in two ways: either as flows over time, or as capital gains.[11] Their distribution depends upon the organisation under which the innovations occurred.[12] Schumpeter usually treats them as being split between entrepreneurs and capitalists, who finance the entrepreneurs' activities.[13]

Schumpeter envisages this process of innovation and adjustment as an interval between successive rational expectations equilibria. He pays great attention to the exact nature of such transitional intervals, for he sees in them the historically specific form of capitalist development, and it is this development which is his chief concern. In Schumpeter's vision innovations are clustered and generate a complicated series of economic cycles.[14] Out of the recovery phase of each cycle a new rational expectations equilibrium is approached, and this sets the stage for a new innovationally inspired boom. Growth in capitalist economies is therefore essentially cyclical. Schumpeter also speculated on the demise of these economies and, more particularly, on how capitalist institutions and cultural values would succumb to those of centralised socialism. This would lead to a different form of economic development.[15]

The Schumpetarian theory of pure profit is based upon the concept of structural change. In his view a capitalist economy with a stable structure of tastes, technology and distribution of assets would result in zero pure profits. Further, structural change generating non-zero pure profits is considered innovational. One can certainly conceive of major changes which would not be encompassed by Schumpeter's notion of innovation. For example, an autonomous change in consumers' tastes could occur. However, he dismisses such possibilities as without empirical importance.[16] More fundamentally, one can seriously question whether structural change is in fact the significant economic phenomenon underlying pure profits. Rather, *unexpected* change would seem to be of primary theoretical importance and this is not necessarily coterminous with structural change. Indeed, Schumpeter himself hints that uncertainty is in fact the relevant principle on which a fully general theory of pure profit ought to be based.[17] It was Knight (1921), however, who explicitly followed up this line of enquiry.

Knight: Uncertainty and Pure Profit

Knight begins his analysis in the same manner as Schumpeter, though there is a significant shift of emphasis. In the sequence of temporary equilibria discussed above, agents forecast equilibrium prices accurately, and Knight concentrates on how this perfect foresight precludes the existence of pure profit.[18] Unlike Schumpeter, he is not concerned to explore the conditions which rationalises such a state of affairs. Instead, he traces the possibility of non-zero pure profits directly to the limited forecasting potentialities inherent in any environment of uncertainty.[19]

The link between uncertainty and non-zero pure profits had in fact been made by many economists prior to Knight.[20] The distinctiveness of his approach lies in the attempt to link pure profits with *particular forms* of uncertainty. He distinguishes between situations of 'risk' and those of 'uncertainty' proper and argues that it is the latter, alone, which allow pure profits to deviate from zero. If 'risk' were the sole form of uncertainty, the situation would be akin to perfect foresight and no pure profits would be possible.

Knight's distinction between 'risk' and 'uncertainty' proper hinges upon whether or not uncertain outcomes can be represented by an 'objective' probability distribution. Where outcomes can be described by such a distribution the condition is classified as one involving 'risk'.[21] Where outcomes cannot be so described, the condition is considered to be one of 'uncertainty'.[22] In the former case, uncertainty is measurable, in the latter case it is not; only vague and subjective estimates of outcomes are possible. Situations of 'risk' arise when there is sufficient data to calculate a probability distribution which would be 'objective' in the sense that all rational agents would accept it as indicating the relative likelihood of outcomes.[23] Situations of 'uncertainty' proper have no such basis from which agreement could arise and agents' estimates of outcomes will be subjective and different.[24]

Uncertain conditions involving 'risk' alone would be associated with zero pure profits. Situations of 'risk' allow accurate prediction of what will happen in 'groups of instances' or 'on the average', and this stochastic form of perfect foresight or rational expectations is sufficient to rule out any pure profits:

> The fact is that while a single situation involving a known risk may be regarded as 'uncertain', this uncertainty is easily converted into effective certainty; for in a considerable number of such cases the results become predictable in accordance with the laws of chance, and the error in such prediction approaches zero as the number of cases is increased. Hence it is simply a matter of an elementary development of business organization to combine a sufficient number of cases to reduce the uncertainty to any desired limits. This is, of course, what is accomplished by the institution of insurance.[25]

Uncertainties proper are inherently non-insurable and are the basis for pure profits:

> Profit arises out of the inherent, absolute unpredictability of things, out of the sheer brute fact that the results of human activity cannot be anticipated and then only in so far as even a probability calculation in regard to them is impossible or meaningless. The receipt of profit in a particular case may be argued to be the result of superior judgement.[26]

According to Knight, the capitalist organisation of economic activity reflects this distinction between risk and uncertainty.

Institutions like insurance develop to handle risks,[27] while a sub-set of agents, entrepreneurs, specialise in meeting uncertainty:

> With uncertainty present, doing things, the actual execution of activity, becomes in a real sense a secondary part of life; the primary problem or function is deciding what to do and how to do it. . . . [Capitalist institutions reflect this. Under this system] a special social class, the business men, direct economic activity; they are in the strict sense the producers, while the great mass of the population merely furnish them with productive services, placing their persons and their property at the disposal of this class; the entrepreneurs *also* guarantee to those who furnish productive services a fixed remuneration.[28]

Knight therefore classifies income into two types; contractual income—interest, wages and rent—and pure profit, which is a residual. Entrepreneurs include those agents who have abilities in estimating uncertain outcomes and also have the confidence to act upon these abilities.[29] On the basis of their 'guesses' they make contracts with other agents for productive services, and thereby *guarantee* these other agents' incomes, which are now certain.[30] Revenues received over and above these costs are pure profits and are dependent upon how well entrepreneurs estimate the consequences of the activities they set in motion.[31] The entrepreneurial pure profits can be conceptualised either as an income flow or as a capital gain.[32]

Knight's thesis, as outlined above, is sharp and clear.[33] Its limitations can also be located precisely. Uncertainty proper is not, in itself, sufficient to preclude full insurance and generate non-zero pure profits. This is shown to be the case by considering the theory of contingent commodities developed by Arrow and Debreu.[34] Furthermore, uncertainty proper is not necessary to preclude insurance. No insurance may be possible for particular activities, even if information on activities were sufficient to estimate the frequency distribution of outcomes with perfect accuracy. The reason for this lies in 'moral hazard'.

The theory of contingent commodities is a development of

the Walrasian theory considered in Chapter 10. It is based upon an extended definition of commodities which allows the whole theory of intertemporal equilibrium to encompass uncertain outcomes, including uncertainty in Knight's sense. The basic aspects of the theory is as follows. Assume an economy extends over a number of periods and at each date in the future the 'state of the world' is uncertain. For example, it may 'rain' or 'not rain'. Agents are assumed to know what states are possible and how each state will affect them but not know what state will actually occur at any future date. In such an economy each dated commodity may play different economic roles according to which states materialise. Consequently, agents will incorporate this into their plans. They will transact for dated commodities whose delivery will be now contingent upon a particular state occurring. All contracts are in the nature of insurances or gambles and demands and supplies reflect agents' estimates of which states will characterise each date, as well as tastes, technology and asset endowments.

All the properties of the Walrasian intertemporal model under certainty hold in this case, except for a reinterpretation required by the enlarged definition of commodities. Consequently, the intertemporal equilibrium of such an economy will involve zero pure profits, despite the existence of a pervasive uncertainty. Furthermore, it is not entrepreneurs or producers who bear the costs of uncertainty. Only consumers have to guess future states and they alone benefit or suffer depending upon how correct their estimates turn out to be. The profits of producers in equilibrium will be invariant to the states which occur. They contract for state-contingent inputs so as to be sure of fulfilling their contracts for state-contingent outputs. Maximisation and competition will ensure zero pure profits, as in the intertemporal equilibrium without uncertainty. Consumers' utility will vary depending upon which states occur and the guesses upon which they made contracts. Those better at guessing will benefit more, other things being equal, than those whose guesses turn out to be poor. However, differences in consumers' welfare are subjective variations in utility levels and have no relevance to pure profits as understood by Knight.

The reasons why such a world involving perfect possibilities for insurance does not exist are related to the reasons whereby a full complement of non-contingent futures markets is absent (see pp. 113–14).[35] However, another reason lies in the phenomenon known as *moral hazard*, and this leads to another fundamental criticism of Knight's theory. Even if the probability distribution of outcomes for particular activities were known with certainty, moral hazard could preclude insurance. For example, imagine there were sufficient data on the history of business success so that one could compute predictively reliable probability distributions of the profit outcomes, for various types of entrepreneurial activities. This is a situation of 'risk' as Knight defines it. However, entrepreneurs would not be able to insure against profits falling below a particular value: 'The insurance policy might itself change incentives and therefore the probabilities upon which the insurance company had relied.'[36] This does not necessarily mean that the act of insurance converts a situation of 'risk' into Knightian uncertainty. The change in probabilities, associated with different insurances, may be known. Nevertheless, the change may be such as to preclude mutually beneficial trade in insurance.[37] This is so quite irrespective of the considerations underlying Knight's distinction between 'risk' and 'uncertainty'.[38]

Market Power and Pure Profits

It is now generally accepted by supply and demand theorists that pure profits arise in part out of superior 'guesswork', which may be associated with what Schumpeter called 'innovations'. Perusal of any elementary textbook will quickly reveal that these beliefs are widespread among neoclassical economists.[39]

Both Schumpeter and Knight considered that these determinants of pure profit worked through an imperfection in competition. Thus, for example, successfully innovating entrepreneurs garnered pure profits via the market power which being 'first in the field' allowed. Schumpeter and Knight, however, considered any particular basis of market power to be temporary. Once knowledge of pure profits, and the cause of their occurrence spread, imitation by other agents would set up forces tending to eliminate them.

There can be no doubt that economic models involving clearly specified market power which is assumed to continue can generate persistent profits above the competitive rate.[40] This has long been accepted by all schools of economists. However, among neoclassical economists especially, there is great disagreement about the plausibility of regarding market power associated with pure profits as persistent.[41] The empirical evidence is not much help in deciding on this issue.[42] Moreover, the matter is plagued by a conceptual confusion over what constitutes a competitive market and market power.

The Walrasian definition of competition (as outlined on p. 76) is precise but of limited value. Since agents are assumed to treat prices as parameters, something other than agents must change prices when the economy is out of equilibrium. The usual procedure is to use a Walrasian *tâtonnement* process. This assumes that an auctioneer operates in all markets. If, for any reason, markets do not clear at the prevailing set of prices, commodities which are in excess demand have their prices raised and commodities in excess supply have their prices reduced, providing their prices are positive. For each commodity, the price changes by a greater amount, the greater is the excess demand or supply. Through these rules a new set of prices is formed and announced by the auctioneer. The process continues until an equilibrium is reached, and no trading is permitted outside of equilibrium.[43] Some actual markets do have a mechanism which closely resembles the *tâtonnement* process; but for most markets it would not apply and it is the agents who change prices. This makes it difficult to preserve the other defining quality of competition in Walrasian theory, i.e. that prices at any instant of time are the same for all agents.[44]

Other neoclassical concepts of competition are much less well defined than the Walrasian.[45] Consequently, it is far from clear exactly what constitutes a deviation away from competition, and therefore manifestations of market power. These difficulties multiply once uncertainty is recognised explicitly and the assumption that agents have complete knowledge of prices is jettisoned. It is then possible to construct models which generate economic phenomena typically associated with non-competitive markets, even though the conditions assumed can be reasonably regarded as 'competitive'.[46]

The Social Role of Pure Profits

The social role of pure profits is not a clear-cut issue, except when these profits arise from persistent market power where barriers preclude competition from operating. In this case, most neoclassical economists, on the grounds of both efficiency and equity, would be predisposed to favour state regulation, unless exceptional circumstances were present to justify otherwise. In the case where pure profits arise out of uncertainty their social role is more ambiguous. One reason for this is that their function is dependent upon the uncertainties from which they arise. Arrow, for example, argues as follows:

> Efficiency is used as a justification for some inequality to the extent that it is necessary to offer incentives to elicit superior performance . . . In the actual capitalist world, it is surely true that not all incomes represent necessary incentive payments . . . A capitalist system is intrinsically marked by uncertainty; the very decentralised nature of the system insures that. The existence of uncertainty creates opportunities for speculation and for the exploitation of differential information. Hence there is room for profits by outguessing others. These profits need not correspond to any net social productivity, but only to a redistribution of rewards, thoroughly analogous to betting on horse races . . . a great deal of speculative profits are unrelated to productivity. Hence, they are to a considerable extent a suitable subject for planned redistribution . . . instead of the chaotic redistribution of the market.[47]

On the other hand, emphasising the considerations brought to the fore by Schumpeter can significantly alter the perspective. In the Schumpetarian vision it is the incentives, provided by the prospect of large profits, which motivate entrepreneurs to innovate and generate the dynamism of capitalism: 'The system is cruel, unjust, turbulent, but it does deliver the goods, and, damn it all, it's the goods that you want.'[48]

Notes to Chapter 13

1. Walras (1874, pt. V)
2. See Arrow and Hahn (1971), Arrow (1974), and Ulph and Ulph (1975).
3. Schumpeter (1912, p. 90). See also Schumpeter (1912, ch. 1).
4. See Samuelson (1943).
5. Schumpeter (1912, p. 66).
6. Schumpeter (1912, pp. 74–8, 81–5, 138).
7. Schumpeter (1912, pp. 110, 131–5; 1939, pp. 106–7, 536; 1954, pp. 896–7). Schumpeter traces the embryo of this theory to Marx and Clark. See Schumpeter (1912, p. 60; 1954, pp. 646, 893–6, 1051).
8. Schumpeter (1912, pp. 197, 209).
9. Schumpeter (1912, pp. 154, 172; 1939, pp. 103–6).
10. Schumpeter (1942, ch. 7).
11. Schumpeter (1912, p. 138; 1954, pp. 896–7).
12. Schumpeter (1939, p. 106).
13. Schumpeter (1912, ch. 3).
14. See especially Schumpeter (1912, ch. 6; 1939).
15. See Schumpeter (1912, pp. 85–6; 1939, pp. 223–4; 1942, 1951).
16. Schumpeter (1912, ch. 1 and pp. 61–5).
17. Schumpeter (1912, chs 1, 2, and p. 173).
18. Knight (1921, pp. 35–8, 147–8, 198, 313–14).
19. Knight (1921, pp. 37–8).
20. See Knight (1921, ch. 2; 1934), Lamberton (1965, p. 47) and Schumpeter (1954, pp. 222, 333–4).
21. Knight (1921, pp. 19, 21, 219).
22. Knight (1921, pp. 231–3).
23. Knight (1921, pp. 47, 214–15, 230, 233).
24. Knight (1921, pp. 231, 310–11).
25. Knight (1921, p. 46).
26. Knight (1921, p. 311; see also pp. 42–3, 174, 198, 212–13, 231–2, 313–14 and ch. 8).
27. Knight (1921, ch. 8).
28. Knight (1921, pp. 268, 271).
29. Knight (1921, pp. 241, 257–60, 268–71, 273–5, 324–5, 350).
30. Knight (1921, pp. 268–71).

31. Knight (1921, pp. 280–1, 362–3). Knight suggests that in aggregate pure profits are negative (pp. 284, 363ff) but he provides no evidence on this.

32. Knight (1921, pp. xxxviii; 1936, p. 463).

33. However, Knight (1921) does recognise continually that his bold dichotomies, in fact, cannot be easily made. He accepts that all knowledge is partial, that the estimated frequencies of future outcomes can never be really 'objective' and subject to precise measurement (pp. 199, 223, 227, 231). Measurement is a matter of degree (pp. 246–7) and more or less informed estimates of consequences resulting from any action can always be made (p. 227). Insurance services are available even when estimates of future outcomes have to build upon a very slender past experience (p. 250). The entrepreneurial activity of uncertainty-bearing is split up and combined with other economic functions (pp. 300, 304, 307, 350, 355). No income is purely contractual or 'certain' and pure profit forms a component of virtually all incomes (pp. 272, 277–8, 290, 366). Yet despite all this fudging, Knight still maintains that the central categories, on which his theory of pure profit is based, retain their validity. Subsequent work in the theory of uncertainty has tended to jettison them. This is particularly the case with respect to Knight's pivotal distinction between risk and uncertainty. For example, Hicks (1931, p. 175) writes:

> Professor Knight's doctrine of 'measurable risks' is one of the parts of his teaching that I am quite unable to accept, at any rate in the uncompromising form in which he first states it (*Risk, Uncertainty and Profit*, pp. 43ff). It is quite true that there are certain kinds of risk that are practically eliminated in a business of reasonable size — Mangoldt's 'Champagnerfabrikant' with his broken bottles is the classical example of this. Experience has shown that the chance of failure is expressible by a definite fraction. But even here the possibility of elimination depends on the size of the business. It will not necessarily be desirable to extend a business beyond what would from other points of view be the optimum size in order to eliminate completely a small risk. Nor will it necessarily be worth while to eliminate such a risk by insurance. Insurance involves costs of administration and it is once more a question of balancing advantages whether these costs should be insured or not.
>
> Further, the grouping of measurable risks is simply a limiting case, and not a very important one, of the general principle of reduction. Reduction is applicable even when experience does not give us sufficient ground for a knowledge of the exact chances. Even Professor Knight himself admits this (ibid, p. 239) and the whole case has been admirably stated by Professor Hardy: 'All applications of the law of averages rest on a grouping of things, unlike in many respects, into classes, on the basis of

certain similarities; if cases nearly alike are infrequent, we must do our grouping on the basis of less homogeneous classes. If the classification is crude, or if the cases are not numerous, the statistical method loses its accuracy. But these cases certainly shade off into Professor Knight's "true uncertainties" by imperceptible degrees, the margin of error getting larger as the evidence gets more scanty.' [G. O. Hardy, *Readings in Risk and Risk Bearing*, University of Chicago Press, 1924, p. 55]

See also Arrow (1971b, pp. 1–43), Weston (1954), and Friedman (1976, pp. 279–82). The criticisms made of Knight in this text do not, however, depend upon rejecting his categories.

34. See Arrow (1953), Debreu (1959, ch. 7), Arrow and Hahn (1971, pp. 122–6), and Radner (1970).
35. See also Arrow (1974).
36. Arrow (1971b, p. 142).
37. See Pauly (1966) and Arrow (1971b).
38. Knight is not unaware of 'moral hazard'. However, he interprets it solely as a factor making for 'uncertainty' and gives it no particular emphasis.
39. See, for example, Samuelson (1973), McConnell and Pope (1981), and Stonier and Hague (1972). See also Hicks (1931), Hahn (1947), Davis (1952), Weston (1954), Bronfenbrenner (1960), and Lamberton (1965).
40. A multitude of partial-equilibrium models can be found in textbooks of microeconomics and industrial organisation. See, for example, Scherer (1971) and Koutsoyiannis (1979). General-equilibrium formulations also exist. See, for example, Negishi (1961), and Arrow and Hahn (1971). However, from a strict neo-classical perspective, these models are unsatisfactory. On this, see especially Roberts and Sonnenschein (1977).
41. More precisely, market power other than labour unions and that sustained by state regulations. See, for example, Goldschmid, Mann and Weston (1974, esp. pt 4).
42. See Goldschmid *et al.* (1974) and Eatwell (1971).
43. See Arrow and Hahn (1971, pp. 264–70).
44. *Tâtonnement* is therefore closely related to the Walrasian definition of competition. But its functions are wider than this. For example, if one wishes to examine the stability of an equilibrium, it is necessary that the equilibrium still exists when the economy is out of equilibrium. If disequilibrium trading were allowed, this could not be assured because the distribution of assets would be changing with prices.
45. See Stigler (1957), Aumann (1964), and Andrews (1964).
46. See Stigler (1957), Alchian (1970), Rothschild (1973), Arrow (1974), and Stiglitz (1975).
47. Arrow (1976, p. 17).
48. Robinson (1964, p. 130).

Part IV
A DOUBLE CRITIQUE

14
Supply and Demand Theories of Profit: A Critique from the Perspective of Surplus Theory

Introduction

Ricardo, Marx, Sraffa and their followers in the surplus tradition have taken a critical stand with regard to supply and demand theories of profit. As we have seen in Part II, equilibrium profits and the rate of profit are determined in the surplus approach by forces other than supplies and demands. The only role which these concepts have is that associated with capital and labour mobility, which are assumed to bring about the uniformities exhibited in 'long-period' states.[1] Concepts of supply and demand are, therefore, relevant only with regard to transitional periods, not to terminal states whose properties are otherwise determined.

One reason why Ricardo and Marx took such a position was their belief that supply and demand theories were empty of definite content. Or, put alternatively, they considered 'an explanatory principle based merely on "demand and supply" was too weak to support the corollaries which a theory of value ought properly enable one to draw'.[2] Furthermore, both Ricardo and Marx were singularly unimpressed with the arguments of their critics who reasoned in terms of supply and demand and they came to identify the defects in their critics' arguments with the concepts in which they were expressed.[3]

Taken in isolation, one should not give undue weight to these views. Although they can be given a rationale which makes them relevant to contemporary neoclassical theories (see pp. 143–4), it is true to say that prior to the last third of the nineteenth century most supply and demand theorists would have been hard pressed to explain exactly what 'supplies' and 'demands' represented. Of greater significance is the critical position which has emanated from the work of Sraffa. This is directly relevant to the more refined and exact theories of supply and demand discussed in Part III. It is made of stronger stuff than anything found in Ricardo and Marx and has had a devastating impact upon Austrian capital theory and the theory of capital productivity. Furthermore, there are some who maintain that a Sraffian critique may be developed to cover *all* theories of supply and demand, including Walrasian theory.

In this chapter the propositions that form the backbone of this critique are outlined. Then we examine how far these propositions apply to Walrasian theory and also consider another possible limitation of this analysis which has been suggested by surplus theorists. Finally, a less concrete, but no less important, issue concerning general neoclassical methodology is discussed.

There is of course a potential problem in using Sraffa's analysis to evaluate profit theories based upon supply and demand. The frameworks are very different, as can be seen by comparing Chapter 2 with Chapter 9. Nevertheless, any difficulties stemming from this are easily surmounted (see pp. 38–40).[4] In this chapter the Sraffa systems used are best interpreted as representing stationary states, where all the capital goods produced simply replace capital goods used up in production. This is the type of equilibrium most commonly employed in Austrian theory and the theory of capital productivity (see above, pp. 99, 104).

Reduction to Dated Labour

Of greatest importance to the evaluation of the Austrian theory of profit is the operation of 'reduction to dated labour' as developed by Sraffa (1960). This is the procedure by which a Sraffian representation of the production process for a commodity is converted into an Austrian form. In other words:

> [Reduction is] an operation by which in the equation of a commodity the different means of production used are replaced with a series of quantities of labour, each with its appropriate 'date'.
>
> Take the equation which represents the production of commodity 'i' . . .
>
> $$(a_{i1}p_1 + a_{i2}p_2 + \ldots + a_{in}p_n)(1 + r) + f_i w = p_i$$
>
> We begin by replacing the commodities forming the means of production of i with their own means of production and quantities of labour; that is to say, we replace them with the commodities and labour which, as appears from their own respective equations, must be employed to produce those means of production; and they, having been expended . . . earlier . . . will be multiplied by a profit factor at a compound rate for the appropriate period, namely the means of production by $(1 + r)^2$ and the labour by $(1 + r)$ . . .
>
> We next proceed to replace these latter means of production with their own means of production and labour, and to these will be applied a profit factor . . . to the means of production $(1 + r)^3$ and to the labour $(1 + r)^2$.
>
> We can carry this operation on as far as we like and if next to the direct labour f_i we place the successive aggregate quantities of labour which we collect at each step . . . we shall obtain the 'reduction equation' for the product in the form of an infinite series [of dated labour components].[5]

Austrians have always expressed production processes in this form without enquiring as to whether it is generally possible to do so. In the case where each commodity is produced by a single process, Sraffa shows that the reduction can be accomplished. Furthermore, he demonstrates that an analysis in terms of a 'reduced' process gives the same results as that applied to the non-reduced process from which it is derived.[6]

In doing so he provides some support for the legitimacy of the Austrian conceptualisation of production as 'a one-way avenue that leads from "factors of production" to "consumption goods".'[7] But the same analysis can be used to directly undermine the generality of this conceptualisation. The source of the difficulty lies in joint production.

Sraffa provides the following example. Assume a system incorporates the following two production processes:

$$(M_0 p_{m0} + a_{11} p_1 + a_{12} p_2 + \ldots + a_{1k} p_k)(1+r) + f_1 w$$
$$= b_{11} p_1 + M_1 p_{m1}$$

$$(M_1 p_{m1} + a_{21} p_1 + a_{22} p_2 + \ldots + a_{2k} p_k)(1+r) + f_2 w$$
$$= b_{21} p_1$$

These production processes are represented as in Chapter 5 except for the terms involving M_0 and M_1: M_0 is a new durable machine required to produce commodity 1 in process 1, and p_{m0} is its price; M_1 is the machine when it is 'one period old', and p_{m1} is its price. In the argument below it is assumed that $b_{11} = b_{21}, f_1 = f_2$ and $a_{1j} = a_{2j}(j = 1, \ldots, k)$. This means that these production processes involve a machine of constant efficiency with a fixed life of two periods. When new, the machine produces b_{11} of commodity 1 and itself one year older. The older machine, in conjunction with the same inputs as are utilised with the new machine, produces the same output of commodity 1, $b_{21}(= b_{11})$.

> The equations for fixed capital make it easy to see how an attempt to effect the 'reduction' of a durable instrument to a series of dated quantities of labour will in general fail ... the first step towards the 'reduction' of the one-year-old machines M_1 to a series of labour terms is to subtract the second equation from the first so as to isolate M_1, leaving it as the sole product on the right-hand side. As a result of this there appears a similar quantity M_1 among the means of production; it has, however, a negative sign and its price is multiplied by $(1 + r)$.
>
> This is by itself sufficient to show that we are engaged in a blind alley: for when we come to the 'reduction' of

the negative term containing M_1, there will appear among its residual means of production a positive M_1; and so, with successive steps, M_1 will constantly reappear, alternately positive and negative, and in each case multiplied by a higher power of $(1 + r)$. This will make it impossible on the one hand for the residual aggregate of commodities to tend to a vanishing-point and on the other for the sum of labour terms to tend to a limit. (This conclusion, based on the assumption of constant efficiency, holds *a fortiori* when the product of a machine diminishes with age; but it would cease to be true and the 'reduction' to dated labour terms, some positive and some negative, would become possible if the annual product were to increase with age.)[8]

Even in the latter case, however, since some of the terms represent negative quantities 'no reasonable interpretation could be suggested'.[9]

There is therefore substance in Sraffa's remark that 'the . . . picture of the system of production and consumption as a circular process . . . stands in striking contrast to the view . . . of a one-way avenue that leads from "factors of production" to "consumption goods".'[10] Not all production structures which can be represented as a set of 'circular' processes can be meaningfully translated into the 'one-way avenue' form. In other words, Wicksell is wrong when he states that all 'capital goods, however different they may appear, can always be ultimately resolved into labour and land'.[11] This strikes at the very foundation of Austrian theory. Without representation in terms of dated original factors none of the superstructure can stand. There is no possibility of measuring roundaboutness and no possibility of associating roundaboutness with other economic categories — accumulation, distribution, or the rate of profit.

Reswitching

In the case where there is no joint production Sraffa's analysis indicates that reduction to dated labour is possible (see pp. 133–4). However, even in this case another aspect of his analysis shows that neither Böhm-Bawerk's average period of production nor any other measure of roundaboutness can play the role assigned to it in Austrian theory. There is no necessary association between a higher degree of roundaboutness, however measured, and a lower r.

In Chapter 5 (pp. 44–5) two simple Sraffa systems were discussed and their $w-r$ curves compared. As represented in Figure 5.2 (p. 45) we have an example of the phenomena called *reswitching*.[12] The outer envelope *abcd* forms the wage–profit frontier. It shows the maximum r associated with any w or the maximum w associated with any r. The same system of production is the most profitable at more than one rate of profit, while another system is more profitable at intermediate rates of profit. Consequently, if system α were more 'roundabout' than system β, a decline in r through r_2 would be in accordance with Austrian theory. But a further decline in r through r_1 would not. The opposite of what Austrian theory proposes occurs. This also undermines the possibility of relating the rate of profit to the marginal productivity of roundaboutness.

This example pertains to systems of production which are represented in a non-Austrian form. However, there is nothing significant in this. Reswitching can be shown to be possible even if attention were explicitly confined to the Austrian representation of technology.[13]

Capital Reversal

Given a wage–profit curve we can deduce certain properties of the Sraffa system from which it is derived. Take, for example, the case of Figure 5.1, which is redrawn as Figure 14.1. Ow_{MAX} measures the wage rate when the rate of profit is zero. As the maximum w possible when only this system is used, it also measures the net physical product per worker when the system is operated in a stationary state, with the consumption good the only net output. Given a wage Ow_1, $w_{MAX} - w_1$ measures the amount of the consumption good received as profit by capitalists per worker employed. Consequently, the tangent of the angle α measures the *value* of

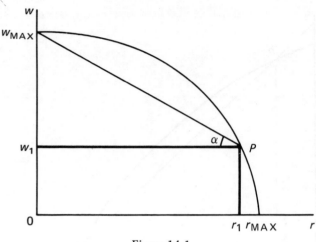

Figure 14.1

capital per worker at the wage rate of w_1. The value of capital per worker is equal to:[14]

$$\frac{\text{Profit per worker}}{r_1} = \frac{w_{MAX} - w_1}{w_1 p} = \tan \alpha$$

Thus in Figure 5.2, which incorporates the w–r curves of two systems, we can now determine the capital intensities of these two systems for all wage rates and rates of profit. These are shown in Figure 14.2. Capital reversal occurs at r_2. It represents the situation where, as there is a change from one system to another with a fall in r, a lower capital intensity (k) occurs. This is clearly contrary to both Austrian pronouncements (see pp. 98–9) and also the theory of capital productivity, which invariably associate a higher capital intensity with a lower r.

Reswitching is always associated with capital reversal, but capital reversal can occur independently of reswitching.[15]

The Marginal Product of Capital and the Rate of Profit

In Chapter 12 it was argued that capital productivity theorists aggregated capital goods into 'capital', through the equilibrium

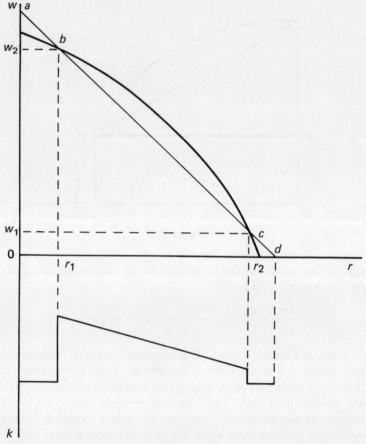

Figure 14.2

prices of these goods, and that this was the appropriate procedure for them to adopt given the results they sought to establish. It was also pointed out (p. 108) that Wicksell had argued that the marginal product of value capital would not equal, in general, the rate of profit. Sraffa's analysis can be used to reaffirm this.

The $w-r$ frontier in Figure 14.2 is made up from the $w-r$ curves of two systems. We now examine the case where the number of systems becomes infinite, such that the magnitude of a change in r, or w, required to move producers from one system to another becomes infinitesimal. In this case the marginal product of capital can be defined as the (limiting) ratio of the increment in the value of output to the increment in the value of capital as the economy moves between systems.[16] It is easily proved using elementary calculus that for such a marginal product to equal the rate of profit, the value of capital per man must be equal to the absolute slope of the $w-r$ frontier at the point of measurement. The following condition must always hold:

$$q = kr + w$$

where q is net output per worker and k is the value of capital per worker. If we take the total differential we obtain:

$$dq = r\, dk + k\, dr + dw$$

and hence we find that the marginal product of capital, dq/dk, is not equal to r unless $k = -dw/dr$.[17] Thus if in Figure 14.3 $ff'f''f'''$ represents the $w-r$ frontier, made up from an infinity of $w-r$ curves like aa' and bb', the marginal product of capital will equal the rate of profit at w^*r^* only if the value of capital per man is equal to $\tan \beta$. However, we know from the $w-r$ curve bb', which contributes the relevant point to the frontier, that the value of capital per worker is equal to $\tan \alpha$. In Figure 14.3 this is not equal to $\tan \beta$. Only in special cases will the two angles be equal and the marginal product of capital be equal to the rate of profit. This result is independent of the occurrence of reswitching and capital reversal. Even if these do not occur, this does not imply that the marginal product of capital will equal the rate of profit.

As we noted in Chapter 12 (p. 108), Wicksell realised that the marginal product of capital would not equal, in general, the rate of profit. But Wicksell failed to perceive the possibility of capital reversal. He erroneously believed that when the equilibrium rate of profit fell the associated changes in prices would always operate in the direction of increasing the magnitude of the pre-existing capital stock. As a consequence, the marginal product of capital is always less than the rate of profit. This belief stemmed from the model which Wicksell used to derive his conclusions: an Austrian point input—point output model in which it is always true that as the rate of

profit falls, capital intensity rises.[18] Wicksell's pupil, Ackerman, did realise that a capital-stock devaluation could occur
as the rate of profit fell and that the marginal product of
capital could be greater than the rate of profit. But Wicksell
himself failed to recognise the implications which this had for
his own analysis.[19] Consequently, he continued to believe
that capital intensity was an inverse function of the rate of
profit. We have already shown that this belief is mistaken.

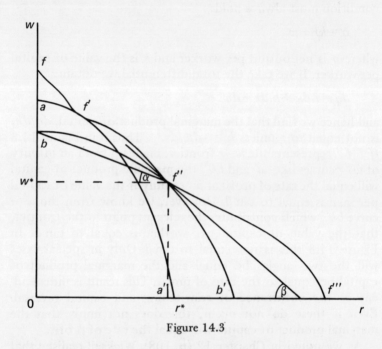

Figure 14.3

The Inverse Relation of the Wage and Rate of Profit

The neoclassical economists discussed in Chapters 11 and 12
shared the belief held by Ricardo and Marx that comparing
equilibria of economies with the same technology would
show an inverse relation between the wage and rate of profit.
Sraffa's analysis indicates that this is not always so.[20]

In Chapter 6 (p. 52) it was pointed out that this result
should not be regarded as 'peculiar'. Nevertheless, the intuitive

understanding provided then was limited. The Austrian conceptualisation of production in terms of dated inputs and dated outputs, however, allows economic understanding to progress beyond this. If in a flow input—flow output process, as represented by expression (11.1) on page 95, output per worker fluctuates so that there are changes in the sign of the terms

$$\left[\frac{b_{i+1}}{f_{i+1}} - \frac{b_i}{f_i} \right]$$

we can consider the producer who operates such a process as engaging in 'borrowing' and 'lending' transactions. When output per worker during a particular period is relatively high, more revenue is received than is absorbed in profit and wage costs. The converse holds when output per worker during a particular period is relatively low. This means that it becomes possible for the producer to gain as a 'lender' from an increase in the rate of profit, given the wage, more than he loses as a borrower. However, since the present value of 'deficits' and 'surpluses', totalled over the whole process, must equal zero under competitive conditions, in this case a higher rate of profit requires a higher wage to be paid, rather than a lower wage.[21]

Walrasian Theory

The results presented so far in this chapter completely undermine the logical coherence of the Austrian theory of profit and the theory of profit based on capital productivity. They can be valid only under restrictive circumstances which rule them out as general theories of profit. The status of Walrasian theory as outlined in Chapter 10, and on the basis of which the theories of Chapter 13 were discussed, is less clear cut. It is also a more important issue. The practitioners of modern Walrasian theory stress its generality. The view, increasingly pervasive among neoclassical economists in the twentieth century, is that Walrasian analysis provides a comprehensive theoretical framework for neoclassical economics as a whole.

In terms of this view, the theory of capital productivity and Austrian theory are seen as involving specialisations of the assumptions lying behind modern Walrasian theory.[22] Thus, if surplus theorists were to expose a flaw in this, the implications for neoclassical theory as a whole, and not just for neoclassical theories of profit, would be immense and far more important than anything else discussed.

None of the results dealt with in the preceeding five sections has relevance for a critique of Walrasian theory. The Austrian representation of technology, in terms of dated original factors producing dated consumption goods, can be incorporated into Walrasian theory. But Walrasian theory is not logically bound to this Austrian conception. Consequently, difficulties posed in reduction to dated labour have no force when applied to Walrasian theory. The possibility of reswitching and of a direct relation between the wage and rate of profit initially came as a surprise to many neoclassical theorists. However, these phenomena do not put into question the logic of Walrasian theorems on comparative statics. Walrasian models can be constructed exhibiting these phenomena.[23] More generally, it is now appreciated that the set of definite comparative-static propositions, generated by the more abstract Walrasian models, is extremely sparse.[24] Capital reversal also poses no problems for Walrasian analysis, because value capital is not a concept in terms of which the theory is constructed.[25] It follows that no concept of the marginal product of capital plays any role either.

Economists in the surplus tradition, however, have laid other criticisms at the door of Walrasian theory. In particular, they have alleged that the concept of intertemporal equilibrium is not a genuine equilibrium, a genuine terminal state. This charge stems from the belief that in a Walrasian intertemporal equilibrium, unlike that of their own 'long-period' equilibrium, embodying the uniformity principle, the rate of return on produced means of production is not equalised. Consequently, the market-clearing conception of Walrasian theory is at most a 'short-period' equilibrium and does not correctly depict the relationship between economic variables in a genuine terminal state.[26]

Clearly, there are differences between the 'long-period' equilibria employed by surplus theorists and the intertemporal market-clearing conception of Walrasians. However, a difference does not lie in Walrasian theory generating unequal rates of return on investments over the same time period. Such inequalities could never characterise a Walrasian intertemporal equilibrium, because the theory on which it is based assumes thoroughgoing maximisation behaviour under competitive and certain conditions. This means that once a *numéraire* is specified, rates of return on different assets over the same time period must be equal when calculated on the basis of *numéraire* values.[27]

It is true that such rates of return are not necessarily akin to the concept of a uniform rate of profit as utilised by surplus theorists. This is because in a Walrasian equilibrium relative prices may change over time, whereas in the long-period equilibrium of surplus theorists, the prices applicable at the input date are the same as those applicable at the output date. The uniform rate of profit in surplus theory is therefore an equal rate of return with stationary prices. The rate of return in Walrasian theory is a rate in a context where prices need not be stationary. The real issue, then, is not one concerning rates of return, but whether or not stationary prices will characterise a terminal state applicable to a capitalist economy. We return to this issue in the next chapter (pp. 149–51).

Methodology

Surplus theory and theories of supply and demand exhibit distinct perspectives. Economic phenomena are incorporated into analysis in very different ways. There is a 'subjectivism' inherent in the neoclassical approach which is absent in surplus theory. All versions of the former concentrate attention upon the decisions or choices of optimising individual agents. Surplus theory, in contrast, seeks to comprehend systemic properties directly, without the intervention of human subjectivities or, if reference is made to such subjectivities, they are assigned no independent causal role but instead are considered to be determined by the nature of the economic system.[28]

This difference is related to wider issues which encompass different views on the status of social theory as 'science', or the kind of social analysis which is possible.[29] It is reflected in Ricardo's statement to Mathus: 'you say demand and supply regulates value – this I think is saying nothing'.[30] Ricardo was interested in developing 'clear cut results of direct practical significance'[31] and he viewed supply and demand analysis as inherently incapable of generating such results. Marx shared the same sentiments. He spoke of economic laws 'working with iron necessity toward inevitable results'.[32] Moreover, he criticised supply and demand theories as 'vulgar' in the sense that they concerned themselves with superficial appearances rather than with the true determining structures, which in his view lay in the social relations of capitalist production and were formalised in the concepts of value and surplus value.[33] Expressed in its strongest form, this view regards individual agents as mere embodiments of systemic functions from which develop impersonal laws.[34]

Modern theorists in the surplus tradition have expressed views about supply and demand theories in the same genre.[35] One can easily appreciate why. Despite its undoubted refinement, all neoclassical theory is based upon individual subjectivities: upon 'tastes', 'goals' and 'expectations'. These can be varied and unstable. This emerges most clearly in the theories already examined in Chapter 13. Here agents' current actions depend crucially upon 'guesses' about an unknowable future. It is not difficult to appreciate why some economists think this represents an insufficiently secure foundation for a social theory which seeks to develop exact laws of economic functioning.

Sympathy with such sentiments does not imply, of course, that we have to accept the theoretical position from which the critics argue. However, it does allow an understanding of why some economists, whose analytical abilities are beyond question, refrain from embracing a neoclassical approach to economic theory in general, and of profit in particular, even when Walrasian theory can be regarded as robust on logical grounds.

Notes to Chapter 14

1. See, for example, Ricardo (1817, pp. 249–51) and Marx (1894, ch. 10).
2. Meek (1977, p. 159).
3. See Schumpeter (1954), Dobb (1973), Meek (1977), and Bradley and Howard (1982b).
4. See also Howard (1980).
5. Sraffa (1960, pp. 34–5). Sraffa's notation has been changed to conform with the usage here. The reason why the series would be infinite is because Sraffa assumes that there is at least one basic commodity.
6. Sraffa (1960, pp. 34–40).
7. Sraffa (1960, p. 93).
8. Sraffa (1960, pp. 67–8).
9. Sraffa (1960, pp. 58–9).
10. Sraffa (1960, p. 93).
11. Wicksell (1901, p. 149).
12. Sraffa (1960, part III).
13. See Samuelson (1966), Nuti (1970) or Howard (1981). Actually Böhm-Bawerk's attention was drawn to the possibility of reswitching by Fisher. However, neither saw its significance for Austrian theory. See Velupillai (1975).
14. The value of capital per worker will change as w and r change. Since the *physical* capital per worker is a constant, the change in *value* reflects the change in p_1 specified by equation (5.7) on p. 43. This is called a 'price-Wicksell effect' and is a particular example of the relations considered by Sraffa (1960, ch. 3).
15. This is shown by Pasinetti (1966), Spaventa (1968) and Bliss (1975, pp. 193–4). The proposition that capital intensity and the rate of profit are always inversely related is also undermined by the analysis of non-basics (above, p. 61).
16. See, however, Pasinetti (1969, esp. pp. 280–1).
17. See Bhaduri (1969).
18. See Wicksell (1901, pp. 172–84).
19. See Wicksell (1923, p. 293).
20. Sraffa (1960, pp. 61–2).
21. Nuti (1970). See Howard (1980) for a numerical example.
22. See, for example, Schumpeter (1954), Koopmans (1957), Samuelson (1962), Arrow and Hahn (1971), Malinvaud (1953), Arrow and Starrett (1973), Burmeister (1974), Klundert and Schaik (1974), Bliss (1975), and Dixit (1977).
23. See, for example, Bliss (1975).
24. See Arrow and Hahn (1971). This means that Pasinetti's criticism of 'traditional' comparative-static propositions cannot be legitimately levelled against modern Walrasian theory. See Pasinetti (1977a, pp. 167–9; 1977b) and Howard (1979, pp. 60–3).

146   *A Double Critique*

25. Garegnani's argument against *all* theories of supply and demand, based upon capital reversal, therefore has no relevance to modern Walrasian theory. See Garegnani (1970a, pp. 270–81) and Howard (1979, pp. 122–7).
26. Eatwell (1976, pp. 95–6; 1982, p. 221). See also Garegnani (1970b; 1976), Roncaglia (1978), Petri (1978), and Walsh and Gram (1980).
27. This, of course, assumes rates of return are defined. See Hirshleifer (1970, ch. 3), Dougherty (1972), or Johnson (1973, pp. 152–6).
28. See Dobb (1973), Meek (1977), and Chapter 2 above.
29. See Schumpeter (1952, pp. 84, 124–5, 134–6, 157; 1954, pp. 85–6, 686, 794, 886–9, 917–19, 1056–8) and Lukes (1968).
30. Ricardo (Works VIII, p. 279). See also Ricardo (1817, pp. 382–5).
31. Schumpeter (1954, pp. 452–3).
32. Marx (1867, pp. 8–9).
33. See Howard and King (1975, pp. 39–45, 52–4).
34. See Howard and King (1975, pp. 25–32) and Althusser (1969).
35. See Garegnani (1973, 1976; 1978a; 1979) and Roncaglia (1978).

15
Surplus Theories of Profit: A Critique from the Perspective of Supply and Demand Theory

Introduction

In the light of the results discussed in the previous chapter, it is clear that any criticism of the surplus approach to profit from a neoclassical perspective must be in terms of the Walrasian variant. Furthermore, some important matters remain subjudice at this stage. This is the case with regard to the 'one at a time' method often employed by surplus theorists and, more particularly, with regard to their treating outputs and employment as determined by factors not systematically related to commodity price determination. From a Walrasian perspective this makes no sense. The latter determines equilibrium quantities at market-clearing levels simultaneously with equilibrium prices, and therefore the same forces determine both. Moreover, the structure of Walrasian theory is such that market-clearing is essential to its notion of a terminal state, whether it be a concept of temporary or intertemporal equilibrium. However, these matters cannot be properly dealt with here because a rationalisation of the surplus methodology has not yet been considered analytically. Nevertheless, there are other issues which Walrasian theory highlights. The most important is a questioning of the uniformity principle which defines the 'long-period' states discussed by surplus theorists. This in turn leads to questioning whether a positive surplus is either necessary or sufficient for the existence of positive profit. Moreover, even if the uniformity principle is accepted, there remains a problem in the determination of uniform prices, rate of profit and the wage within the surplus approach.

Before considering these criticisms, however, it is opportune to note the conception of supply and demand theory held by some contemporary surplus theorists.

The Surplus Theorists' Conception of Neoclassical Theory

In the preface to the *Production of Commodities by Means of Commodities* Sraffa states that it is 'a peculiar feature of the set of propositions now published that, although they do not enter into any discussion of the marginalist theory of value and distribution, they have nevertheless been designed to serve as a basis for a critique of that theory'.[1]

The notable aspect of this quotation is that the phrase 'the marginalist theory of value and distribution' is exceedingly vague. However, if we take its terms seriously, there is no way in which modern Walrasian analysis would form part of the theory Sraffa aimed to attack. Modern Walrasian theory is not marginalist. Marginal concepts are not required in its formulation, and, although the relationships holding in an equilibrium of demands and supplies can sometimes be expressed in marginalist terms, there is no need to do so. There is, however, considerable evidence to suggest that those theorists who have sought to undermine *all* forms of neoclassical economics on the basis of Sraffa's work have not realised this. For example, Garegnani defines 'modern value and distribution theory' as

> theory based on the marginal method that has held almost undisputed sway over economic thought since the last quarter of the nineteenth century. At its heart lie the twin concepts of 'marginal utility' (i.e. the increment of satisfaction derived from a unit-increment of consumption of a particular good) and 'marginal product' (i.e. the increase in

output associated with a unit-increment of the 'factor of production' applied).[2]

This view is by no means exceptional.[3] It follows that the Sraffa-based critics of Walrasian theory have a fundamental misconception as to the nature of the theory they seek to undermine. It should therefore come as no surprise if they have failed to appreciate its strengths.

The Uniformity Principle

The conception of equilibrium utilised by all surplus theorists is defined by the uniformity principle. Neoclassical economists, on the other hand, define equilibrium by market clearance. Nevertheless, prior to the 1930s it was generally believed that market clearance implied the uniformity principle and virtually all supply and demand theorists dealt with equilibrium in this form.[4] If the economy is competitive and there is no uncertainty or externalities, then selfish optimising will ensure that over any period homogeneous units of labour receive the same wage, and rates of return will be equal in an equilibrium of supplies and demands. However, there is no assurance that equilibrium prices will be stationary in the sense portrayed by the uniformity principle (that is, in neoclassical terms, stationary *spot* prices). Prices will be determined by the requirement of market clearance, and in general this will require non-uniform prices.

There are particular circumstances in which uniform or stationary prices can characterise an equilibrium defined by market clearance. The most important, historically speaking, is a stationary state. In such a case it is always possible to find a stationary set of prices which will maintain the trades of such an equilibrium. This is also true if the equilibrium is a steady state.[5] Since early Austrian economists and theorists of capital productivity generally confined attention to such equilibria, the use of the uniformity principle was not inappropriate. Apart from these cases little can be said *a priori* about the pattern of equilibrium prices. However, if a presumption is to be made, Walrasian theory suggests that prices will be non-stationary. The reasons for this were discussed in Chapter 10.

Surplus theories incorporate a different structure of causation from supply and demand theory. Here, a distributional variable, either the wage or rate of profit, is taken to be exogenous. This means that surplus theorists can assume directly that either wages or rates of profit are uniform, and the assumption of competition will ensure uniformity in the endogenous distributional variable. However, prices are also considered to be endogenous variables, and assuming competition will not guarantee that these prices are uniform. Moreover, suprlus theorists have not provided any other mechanism by which this result may be guaranteed:

> This is by no means a tangential issue. We can illustrate its significance through the use of a simple Sraffa model. Take, for example, the following system involving one circulating capital good (Commodity 1) and one consumption good (Commodity 2):
>
> $$a_{11}p_1^1(1+r) + f_1 w = p_1^2$$
> $$a_{21}p_1^1(1+r) + f_2 w = p_2^2$$
>
> The superscripts on prices refer to time. Thus p_1^2 is the price of the capital good at the output date and p_1^1 is the price of the capital good at the date when inputs are applied. Assuming that the uniformity principle applies to prices and that the consumption good is taken as *numéraire*, the wage and prices are determined for any specified r. For example, if f_1, f_2, a_{21} are all equal to unity and $a_{11} = 1/5$, then given $r = 1$, w is determined at 3/13 and p_1 at 5/13. But if prices are unconstrained to be uniform, then specifying r and the *numéraire* is not sufficient to determine either prices or the wage. Now, if r is set at unity, the parameters of the numerical example are consistent with $w = 5/13$, $p_1^1 = 4/13$ and $p_1^2 = 33/65$, as well as the previous solution and host of other solutions.[6]

Without the property of stationary prices other propositions established by surplus theorists are threatened. For example, there is no longer any assurance that varying the wage, as in Figure 5.2 (p. 45), will occasion the change of systems deduced upon the basis of assuming stationary prices. Moreover, without the uniformity principle, the link of profit to surplus is severed.

Profit and Surplus

Let us assume a 'one-commodity' economy whose technology is represented by

$$a_{11} + f_1 \rightarrow b_{11} \tag{15.1}$$

Further assume that $a_{11} > b_{11}$ so that no surplus is possible. In this case, if prices are constrained to be uniform, there can be no positive rate of profit even if wages are zero. The rate of profit is given by the equation

$$r = b_{11}/a_{11} - 1 \tag{15.2}$$

Since $b_{11}/a_{11} < 1, r < 0$.

The point to notice is that this result is not brought about by the assumption that the surplus is non-positive; it arises from assuming that prices are stationary. Once this is abandoned nothing can be deduced about the rate of profit from the fact that the surplus is non-positive. In this case the rate of profit is given by the equation

$$r = b_{11}/a_{11} \times p_1^2/p_1^1 - 1 \tag{15.3}$$

and clearly depends upon the price of the commodity at the output date relative to the price at the input date. Thus a positive surplus is not a necessary condition for profits to be positive.

We can also use a similar example to show that even if a physical surplus exists, this is not sufficient to guarantee positive profits. Again, let us assume an economy whose technology is given by relation (15.1). However, now assume $a_{11} < b_{11}$. In this case, with zero wages and prices stationary, equation (15.2) shows that $r > 0$. But if prices cease to be uniform, equation (15.3) indicates that nothing can be deduced from the fact that the surplus is positive; p_1^1 could be sufficiently large relative to p_1^2 to ensure $r < 0$.

These two examples illustrate that what links profits to surplus is stationary prices. Once this assumption is dropped the link is broken. In the absence of any rationale for believing a terminal state will exhibit stationary prices, there is no rationale for concentrating upon surplus as the key to profit.

Determination

Walrasian analysis also suggests that the method of determination utilised in surplus theories of profit is economically suspect. We can again use a very simple example as an illustration. Let us assume that the technology of an economy is represented by

$$a_{11} + f_1 \rightarrow b_{11} + b_{12} \tag{15.4}$$

If we write this system in price terms, assuming stationary prices, we have

$$a_{11}(1 + r)p_1 + f_1 w = b_{11}p_1 + b_{12}p_2 \tag{15.5}$$

Clearly, defining the *numéraire* and taking the wage or the rate of profit as exogenous is not sufficient to allow the determination of the endogenous variables. There will remain two unknowns and only one equation.

The problem here is that the number of processes is less than the number of produced commodities. Sraffa explicitly assumes that the number of processes is exactly equal to the number of commodities.[7] Such an equality is generally implicit in the work of Ricardo and Marx, and other surplus theorists also adhere to it.[8] However, as in the case of stationary prices, no general and convincing rationale has been provided to explain why technology should not be such that the number of commodities exceeds the number of processes.

Dual Price Determination

In the work of Ricardo and Marx, equilibrium profits and prices are determined by forces other than those of supply and demand. However, supplies and demands, through the medium of capital and labour mobility, were appealed to as forces leading the economy to converge upon equilibria. The same duality in the determination of 'short-run' or 'market' prices and 'long-period' or 'normal' prices is manifest in the work of contemporary surplus theorists.[9] This is unsatisfactory for three reasons. First, there is no specific conceptualisation of demands and supplies. In particular, it is not made clear whether they are conceived as Walrasian or non-Walrasian. However, in the light of the considerations dealt with above (pp. 147–8), it would appear that the supplies and demands would be non-Walrasian. In this case some formal specification would be desirable but has not been forthcoming. Second, surplus theorists are prone to assume convergence upon long-period states rather than deduce it from the dynamics of disequilibria.[10] Third, dual price determination sits uneasily with a hostility to supply and demand theories. If demands and supplies are conceived to operate in disequilibria so as to bring about long-period 'centres of gravity', then these equilibria can obviously be represented as being determined by supplies and demands.

Subjectivities

Neoclassical economists are not renowned for delving into methodology. Nevertheless, there can be no doubt that most would see the position outlined on page 143 of the previous chapter as tantamount to a retreat into mysticism. There is a deep and enduring commitment among neoclassical economists to building economics upon the foundation of individual actions. This is taken to involve constructing analysis upon subjectivities. Sometimes short cuts are taken and the principle is held in abeyance. None the less, the legitimacy of the principle is stridently proclaimed. Indeed, the success of the critique against non-Walrasian theory, which was discussed in the preceeding chapter, would reinforce this disposition. The defects in the Austrian theory of profit and the theory of capital productivity can be interpreted as arising in great part from a lack of attention being paid to microeconomic relations.

A rationale for these sentiments is not difficult to spell out. Stated assertively and briefly it could run as follows:

Economic systems essentially consist of the activities of individual economic agents. Consequently, there can be no proper account of causation independent of agents' actions. Furthermore, these actions frequently involve genuine 'choices'. In this sense the economic world is not a simple extension of the natural world.

It is true that neither economists nor other social theorists know very much about how agents form expectations. This is related to the fact that the concept of rational action becomes unclear in situations where the outcomes of any action is not certain. However, there is no justification in searching for causation independently of these subjectivities, particularly when the theory, as developed so far, indicates their pivotal role in determining economic phenomena.

No doubt, neoclassical theory in its present state is guilty of an unwarranted one-sided emphasis in abstracting from the historical contexts in which agents act, and also in overstressing the egoism of agents. Even so, important results have been developed. Moreover, there is no difficulty, in principle, of accepting that preferences, objectives and expectations are socially formed. Furthermore, although there will remain great difficulties in fully accounting for differences in subjective variables, this is reflected in the performance of economies. For example, it is still very much an open question as to why some are dynamic, innovative and profitable, while others are relatively stagnant. Different resource endowments are not without significance, but the historical record shows them to be far from setting binding constraints. Rather, one may hypothesise that it is subjective phenomena — agents' choices and the expectations they entertain as to the consequences of change — that are of significance.

The case rationalising the neoclassical perspective could be continued and polished. However, enough has been stated to indicate, quite irrespective of the critical points raised in the previous sections, why many neoclassical economists would not be satisfied with the way surplus theorists abstract from agents' decisions. In short, between the two traditions there is a difference in vision, and this is naturally reflected in the contents of theory, including theories of profit.

Notes to Chapter 15

1. Sraffa (1960, p. vi).
2. Garegnani (1978b, p. 71).
3. For example, see Roncaglia (1977; 1978), Harcourt (1972), and Pasinetti (1969; 1974; 1977a).
4. See Garegnani (1976), Milgate (1979), and Eatwell (1982).
5. See Bliss (1975) and Dixit (1977).
6. Bradley and Howard (1982c, pp. 245−6; see also pp. 247−8). The notation has been changed to conform with the usage here.
7. Sraffa (1960, pp. 5, 7, 44, 63, 77−8).
8. See, for example, Pasinetti (1980a).
9. See, for example, Garegnani (1976; 1978a; 1979), and Harcourt (1982).
10. See, for example, Eatwell (1976, pp. 95−6).

Part V

PROFIT IN EFFECTIVE DEMAND THEORY

16
Profit and Effective Demand

Theories of Effective Demand

The defining quality of all theories of effective demand is adherence to the proposition that the value of aggregate demand need not equal the value of aggregate supply. More particularly, all of these theories seek to establish the possibility of effective demand failures, i.e. states of the economy in which there is a negative value of aggregate excess demand, which represents underutilised or unemployed inputs. Beyond this, theories of effective demand exhibit few other common threads. However, the key proposition common to all of these theories is of sufficient importance in itself, both for economics as a whole and for the theory of profit, to regard them as a group distinct from those already considered.

Their general importance for economic theory arises primarily because they contradict propositions derived from the theories of supply and demand discussed in Part III and which are still the prevailing force in economics. Naturally this has implications for the determinants of profit, and the role which profits play in a capitalist economy. Once effective demand failures are recognised as significant, it is no longer acceptable to conclude that the determinants of profit lie predominantly in tastes and technology, or, more specifically, in time preference and investment productivity. It is true that the break with neoclassical theories is not total. Most forms of effective demand theory lay stress upon the importance of expectations as a pivotal factor governing economic performance, including the level of profits. This dovetails with the dominant note in

Schumpeter and Knight. However, acceptance of the possibility of effective demand failures implies the rejection of the Walrasian basis to which these theories adhere. Thus, while it would be possible for effective demand theorists to accept the same focus as these neoclassical theorists, the implications which expectations have for the functioning of a system based upon profitability would be seen very differently.

The history of economic thought is replete with economists who have sought to establish the possibility of effective demand failures.[1] Nevertheless, it has become conventional to use the term 'Keynesian theory' as a synonym for theories of effective demand. The rationale for doing so is that the considerations Keynes (1936) raised are deemed to be the most powerful in establishing the principle of effective demand. Nevertheless, neoclassical theory has proved a tougher nut to crack than both Keynes and Keynesians initially expected. The reasons for this are discussed in the next chapter. Here we proceed directly to construct a simple example showing the relationship between effective demand and profits. It assumes, without justification, that the notion of effective demand and effective demand failures are meaningful concepts. We seek only to give a provisional indication of what is at stake for theories of profit.

Profits and Capitalists' Expenditure

Let us assume an economy composed of only two classes, capitalists and workers, and examine the income—expenditure relations assuming workers do not save and that there are sufficient unemployed resources to allow a variation in economic activity without price changes. The following relationship must hold between income and expenditures:

$$Y = P + W = I + C_C + C_W \tag{16.1}$$

Y is national income, P is profits, W is wages, I is net investment, C_C is capitalists' consumption and $C_W (= W)$ is workers' consumption. It follows from (16.1) that

$$P = I + C_C \tag{16.2}$$

Thus profits are equal in magnitude to capitalists' expenditure.

The reason for this is easy to understand. In the case where I and C_C are zero, equation (16.2) indicates that profits are zero. The total net revenue of firms is workers' consumption expenditure, C_W, which is equal to W, the wage costs of production. This means that capitalists in aggregate can only receive profits if there is expenditure which does not arise from costs of production. In this simple model profits are therefore equal to the expenditure of capitalists.

In the case where workers saved, equation (16.1) would yield

$$P = I + C_C - W_S \qquad (16.3)$$

where W_S is workers' saving and is equal to $W - C_W$. Equation (16.3) shows that workers' savings detract from profit. They represent a reduction in aggregate demand without a corresponding reduction in costs of production.

Nevertheless, equations (16.2) and (16.3) imply no causation. This has to be imposed. A typical Keynesian interpretation is one which stresses that the I and C_C components of effective demand determine P. For example, Kalecki, assuming workers' savings are zero, refers to (16.2), and reasons as follows:

> What is the significance of this equation? Does it mean that profits in a given period determine capitalist consumption and investment, or the reverse of this? The answer to this question depends on which of these items is directly subject to decisions of capitalists. Now it is clear that capitalists may decide to consume and invest more in a given period than in the preceding one, but they cannot decide to earn more. It is, therefore, their investment and consumption decisions which determines profits and not vice versa.[2]

Keynes implied adherence to the same direction of causation when he wrote:

> There is one peculiarity of profits (or losses) which we may note in passing, because it is one of the reasons why it

is necessary to segregate them . . . as a category apart. If entrepreneurs choose to spend a portion of their profits on consumption (and there is, of course, nothing to prevent them from doing this), the effect is to increase the profit . . . by an amount exactly equal to the amount of profits which have been thus expended . . . Thus, however much of their profits entrepreneurs spend on consumption, the increment of wealth belonging to entrepreneurs remains the same as before. Thus profits, as a source of capital increment for entrepreneurs, are a widow's cruse which remains undepleted however much of them may be devoted to riotous living. When, on the other hand, entrepreneurs are making losses, and seek to recoup these losses by curtailing their normal expenditure on consumption, i.e. by saving more, the cruse becomes a Danaid jar which can never be filled up; for the effect of this reduced expenditure is to inflict on the producers . . . a loss of an equal amount. Thus the diminution of their wealth, as a class, is as great, in spite of their savings, as it was before.[3]

In other words, the Keynesian interpretation is one which stresses that the effective demand represented by capitalist expenditures is exogenous, and can, therefore, be seen as a determinant of profits, which are endogenous. The rationale for this lies in the belief that current investment is determined by expected future profits, not by current profits. In addition, the assets available to capitalists allows these agents to consume independently of their current incomes to a qualitatively different degree compared with workers. This second factor, however, is generally considered to be less important than the former.

Capitalists' consumption expenditures could be made a function of their current incomes without undermining the substance of this Keynesian interpretation. It is the autonomy of investment which is considered crucial. An increase in effective demand from a rise in investment, resulting from greater entrepreneurial optimism as to the prospect of future profits, would generate increased current profits. The larger effective demand would absorb unemployed resources and outputs would increase. The magnitude by which employment and output increase is that which is sufficient to increase profits by an exact equivalent amount to the increase in capitalists' expenditures. (This is equivalent to saying that output increases until there occurs an increase in savings which exactly equals the increase in investment.) Keynesians therefore regard capitalists' incomes 'as being the resultant of their expenditure decisions, rather than the other way around — which is perhaps the most important difference between "Keynesian" and "pre-Keynesian" habits of thought'.[4]

Conclusion

Pre-Keynesian habits of thought are not homogeneous, as we have seen in previous chapters. In the light of these, it is clear that it is Walrasian analysis which poses the real difficulty to accepting effective demand theory. A Walrasian economist would not question equations (16.1), (16.2) and (16.3). However, the interpretation just outlined would be questioned because it is incompatible with Walrasian theory. This neoclassical analysis implies that the value of aggregate demand is always equal in value to that of aggregate supply. Thus the pivotal role of effective demand, on which the profit theory just described rests, is emasculated. For example, a 'quick and dirty' Walrasian assessment of the theory presented here might go as follows. It is true that equations (16.2) and (16.3) hold, for they are no more than national income identities. The causal interpretation of these equations is flawed in that the value of aggregate demand cannot be less than the value of aggregate supply. Therefore, any increase in capitalists' investment must be matched by a contraction of capitalist consumption or a rise in workers' saving. Consequently, there would be no rise in current profits, as equations (16.2) and (16.3) make clear.

Notes to Chapter 16

1. See, for example, Keynes (1936, ch. 23), Schumpeter (1954), and Blaug (1978).
2. Kalecki (1971, pp. 78–9).
3. Keynes (1931, vol. I, p. 139).
4. Kaldor (1956, p. 369).

17
Effective Demand

Introduction

All forms of neoclassical theory deny the possibility of effective demand failures. In the next section we examine the reasons for this. The focus of attention is on Walrasian theory, which (as we have already seen in Part III) is the most refined product of neoclassical theorising. A denial of the possibility of effective demand failures does not imply, however, a denial of the phenomena conventionally identified as unemployment. This will be explained in the section following.

Obviously, any economics utilising a notion of effective demand must undermine neoclassical theory in some way, so we subsequently examine traditional Keynesian arguments on this issue. They prove to be rather weak. Nevertheless, there does exist stronger material from which effective demand theory can be formulated. This forms the topic of the later sections.

Walras's Law

Let us assume a market economy in which there are n commodities and re-examine the structure of Walrasian demands and supplies. The value of aggregate demand would be given by the expression

$$p_1 D_1 + p_2 D_2 + \ldots + p_n D_n = \sum_{i=1}^{n} p_i D_i \qquad (17.1)$$

where $p_i(i = 1, \ldots, n)$ is the price of commodity i and $D_i(i = 1, \ldots, n)$ is the sum of agents' demands for commodity i. The value of aggregate supply is defined analogously by the expression

$$p_1 S_1 + p_2 S_2 + \ldots + p_n S_n = \sum_{i=1}^{n} p_i S_i \qquad (17.2)$$

where $S_i(i = 1, \ldots, n)$ represents the sum of agents' supplies of commodity i.

The D_i and S_i therefore represent the market demands and supplies of agents who plan in accordance with the neoclassical assumptions. Consumers choose maximal consumptions subject to budget constraints and producers maximise profits subject to technological constraints. With these behavioural patterns it is easy to show that for any set of prices, not just an equilibrium set of prices, the magnitudes of (17.1) and (17.2) must be equal.

The value of producers' demands differs from the value of their supplies by an amount equal to profits. If consumers are *non-satiated*, so that they exhaust their budgets,[1] the value of their demands will equal the value of the assets they supply, including labour services, plus the value of profits which they receive from firms (it being assumed that consumers own firms). Consequently, the value of their demands differs from the value of their supplies by an amount exactly equal to that of producers. However, the differences are of opposite sign, so that when agents are taken all together, the value of aggregate demand is equal to the value of aggregate supply. Thus we have

$$\sum_{i=1}^{n} p_i D_i = \sum_{i=1}^{n} p_i S_i \qquad (17.3)$$

or

$$\sum_{i=1}^{n} p_i E_i = 0 \qquad (17.4)$$

where $E_i(i = 1, \ldots, n)$ is the excess demand for commodity i, defined by $D_i - S_i$.

The expression (17.3), or (17.4), is known as *Walras's law* (sometimes also called *Say's law*). As we have seen, this follows from three apparently weak assumptions: namely, that consumers maximise subject to budget constraints, that no consumer is satiated and that producers maximise profits subject to constraints of technology. Its implications are, however, not weak. It means that the structure of neoclassical theory precludes the possibility of there ever being an effective demand failure.

Unemployment in Neoclassical Theory

Both a Walrasian intertemporal equilibrium and a Walrasian temporary equilibrium involve all markets clearing. There may be an excess supply of particular commodities but they would have a price of zero (see p. 80). These commodities are most appropriately termed redundant rather than unemployed. There will be no unemployment in the sense of there being resources in excess supply at positive prices.

This is a non-controversial conclusion. However, its empirical implications are not clear cut. Neoclassical economists have never denied the possibility of unemployment as conventionally perceived. They have traced its cause to frictions and imperfections in the operation of markets[2], and today there are those, of whom Friedman is the most eminent, who maintain that appropriately specified concepts of Walrasian equilibrium can explain phenomena which are usually identified as unemployment (these economists are frequently referred to as 'monetarists' or 'new classicals' or the 'Chicago school'). In other words, their argument is that if the notion of equilibrium approximates sufficiently closely to the conditions of actual economies, then economic phenomena frequently conceived as unemployment can exist in equilibrium, and equilibrium theory can explain their determinants. In examining this argument, we shall concentrate upon the unemployment of labour but the ideas are easily generalised.

The determining structure of real market economies is conceived to be comprised primarily of tastes, technology, asset ownership and government policies. This structure determines the phenomena observed in such economies. However, the determination is a stochastic one. Economic variables, like market prices, reflect the structure but not in a completely deterministic way. Instead, these variables show random disturbance and their values can be accurately forecast only 'on the average'. Thus it is only possible to know the probability with which a particular variable will take a specific value. It is not possible to predict with complete certainty.

Consequently, the empirically relevant concept of equilibrium is that of a rational expectations Walrasian temporary equilibrium (see pp. 112–15). As a temporary equilibrium, all currently operating markets clear, and as a rational expectations equilibrium, agents' price expectations are, 'on the average', correct. Thus in such an equilibrium the expected frequency distribution of future market-clearing prices held by agents is the distribution which will be actually encountered if the structure remains unchanged. Such an economy can experience fluctuations in real and monetary variables but all agents are adjusted to this. Consequently, the path of an economy in a sequence of rational expectations Walrasian equilibria would be approximated by a Walrasian intertemporal equilibrium.

A rational expectations Walrasian equilibrium is the appropriate conception of equilibrium because it is a terminal state. It represents a situation in which all agents are accommodated to the structure of the economy, in the sense that markets clear and the probabilities assigned to events by different agents are consistent and correct so there is no element of *systematic* error in expectations.

In this state there are no positively priced commodities in excess supply. However, there may be phenomena which convention or policy identifies as unemployment. For example, stochastic variability in commodity markets may be reflected in labour markets. Old workers will be retiring and new workers entering the labour force. Some existing workers will be relocating occupationally. Market imperfections, such as unions and minimum wage laws, can result in unduly low competitively determined wage rates. All of these processes may involve periods of temporary idleness, search for alternative employment and permanent abstention from work, all of which, on the basis of conventional definitions, are classified as unemployment.

This unemployment is often called 'natural', using the term in the Wicksellian sense of referring to equilibrium. Thus, for example, Friedman writes:

> The 'natural rate of unemployment' . . . is the level which would be ground out by the Walrasian system of general equilibrium equations, provided there is embedded in them the actual structural characteristics of the labour and commodity markets, including market imperfections, stochastic variability of demands and supplies, the costs of gathering information about job vacancies and labour availabilities, the costs of mobility, and so on.[3]

The natural rate can change if the structure of the rational expectations Walrasian equilibrium changes.[4] Moreover, deviations from the natural rate can occur if agents do not adjust to the new structure instantaneously. Friedman is fond of locating the major cause of such changes in monetary shocks.[5] For example, imagine for simplicity that the initial equilibrium is a stationary state with a constant price level. If a monetary contraction takes place, according to Friedman's monetary theory, money wages and wage expectations will be required to take lower values in the new equilibrium.[6] If this is not immediately recognised by workers, they will interpret the money wage reductions they encounter as a reduction in real wages. This will occasion substitution into search activities, leisure, etc.,[7] and will be reflected in a rise in recorded unemployment.

'Unemployment' is higher because workers have mistaken a fall in absolute prices for a change in relative prices. They do so because they lack system-wide information on the basis of which new 'rationally expected' prices can be immediately determined.[8] They only have detailed knowledge about the sectors of the economy in which they operate and it is this tunnel vision which allows workers in general to confuse changes in money prices for changes in relative prices. It will take time for the market opportunities subjectively percieved by workers to coincide with the objective market situation, as workers learn new forecasting rules which give results consistent with the new structure. Until they do so, expectations will be incorrect 'on the average' and they will misallocate their resources.

Unemployment above the natural rate is a disequilibrium phenomenon in the sense that it reflects that the economy is away from a terminal state, i.e. is not in rational expectations Walrasian equilibrium. However, the unemployment is an equilibrium phenomenon in the sense that agents are optimising, on the basis of the information they have,[9] and markets are always cleared. There is no 'effective demand failure' and Friedman's view is that expectations will automatically correct themselves quickly to reflect the new structure. This view is widely held by those who adhere to this form of neoclassical unemployment theory.[10]

Effective Demand Failures: The Traditional Arguments

Many theorists who have played a major role in the formalising of modern Walrasian theory have not been impressed with the application of this theory to explain unemployment. Their own view as to the status of Walrasian theory is to emphasise its counterfactual usefulness (see pp. 85–6),[11] and their suspicion of the theory outlined in the preceeding section derives in part from the fact that it treats the results of formal Walrasian theory in a most cavalier fashion. These results show that the existence of unique and stable equilibria can only be guaranteed on very stringent assumptions which are unlikely to be fulfilled in actual economies.[12] Disbelief that Walrasian theory is the appropriate path along which an understanding of unemployment should progress is also buttressed by historical experience. Some economists have viewed with incredulity the work of those who would seek to explain the heavy and persistent unemployment in the 1930s with models in which markets continually clear.[13]

It is true, nevertheless, that traditional Keynesian arguments used to account for effective demand failure are theoretically weak. Viewed in the light of Walrasian theory, they simply will not bear the weight placed upon them.

One such argument is associated with Robinson. It maintains that Keynes saw 'clearly that to recognise that the future is unknown brings down the whole structure of orthodox theory'.[14] It is true that Keynes (1937) perceived Knightian uncertainty to be pervasive in market economies. However, it is not true that this in itself is a decisive objection to Walrasian theory, as we have seen in Chapter 13.

More commonly expressed arguments focus upon the role of liquidity preference in maintaining interest rates 'too high' and on interest-inelastic investment. It is argued that, due to speculative expectations, money can become the preferred asset at rates of interest above the level required for full employment. Furthermore, even if it were possible for money rates of interest to fall to zero, investments may not be sufficiently interest-sensitive so as to ensure complete utilisation of resources. These arguments have become the standard fare of intermediate macroeconomic texts. In terms of the typical *ISLM* model they can be represented by Figures 17.1 and 17.2 respectively, where Y_F represents full-employment output. By themselves, these arguments have no force against Walrasian theory, and therefore no substance in accounting for effective demand failures. Both arguments relate to the functional form of particular aggregate demand relationships and this is not an issue which threatens the existence of Walrasian equilibria. The continuity of demand and supply relationships is

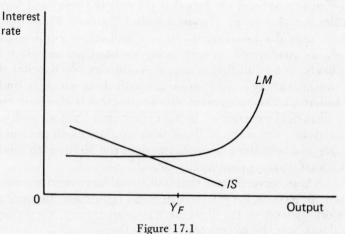

Figure 17.1

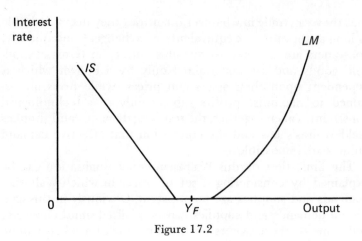

Figure 17.2

another matter (see pp. 80—1) but discontinuities play no role in the typical presentation of these arguments.

Undoubtedly, the most popular argument employed to account for effective demand failures concerns downwardly rigid money wage rates which are too high to ensure full employment. Nevertheless, by itself this argument is powerless to do so. Even if it is accepted that such rigidities characterise all labour markets, this is not sufficient to provide a rationale for effective demand failures. The reason lies in Walras's law, outlined above. One implication of this is that an excess supply of any commodity with a positive price will be balanced by an equivalent value of excess demand in other markets. (If in equation (17.4) it is assumed that some $E_i < 0$ with positive prices, then there must be other $E_i > 0$ since $\Sigma_i p_i E_i = 0$.) Consequently, there is no effective demand failure.

The problem with all these arguments is that they seek to question Walrasian results without questioning the Walrasian conceptualisation of demands and supplies upon which these results rest.

Quantity Constraints

In Walrasian theories of competitive economies, agents are assumed to formulate their demands and supplies in the belief that they can trade in whatever quantities they deem desirable as long as they provide equivalents in exchange. Consequently, consumers are assumed to maximise utility in terms of available goods and are constrained only by a budget which is dependent upon their assets and prices, while firms are assumed to maximise profits subject only to a technological constraint. Taken together, the resulting demands and supplies yield Walras's law and the conclusion that effective demand failures are impossible.

The limitation of this Walrasian conceptualisation can be explained by considering a set of prices in which Walrasian demands and supplies are inconsistent. Obviously in this case not all demands and supplies can be realised simultaneously, and some of those agents on the long side of markets will be rationed if trades actually occur at these prices. (The *tâtonnement* mechanism, as we have seen on page 123, assumes trades will not take place. However, this is an obviously unreasonable characterisation of actual market behaviour.) In these circumstances it is not unreasonable to hypothesise that agents will develop expectations as to the probability of rationing in the future. If these probabilities are non-zero, this will affect other demands and supplies. For example, a consumer who is quantity-rationed in the sale of labour and expects this to continue at future dates will not necessarily change his or her willingness to supply labour from that specified by Walrasian theory, but is likely to reduce demand for currently available consumption goods. A firm which is quantity-rationed in the sale of its output and expects this to continue at future dates will not necessarily change its willingness to supply output from that indicated by Walrasian theory, but is likely to reduce demand for currently available labour. From this, there follows a number of important implications.

First, there are now two types of demand and supply. There are Walrasian demands and supplies which, following Clower (1965), are frequently called 'notional' demands and supplies. There are also quantity-constrained demands and supplies which depend, like notionals, upon prices, budgets and technology but also, unlike notionals, upon quantity constraints operative now or expected to be operative in the future. This means that a concept of effective demands and supplies becomes meaningful. Take the two examples of the previous paragraph. In the case of the consumer, his or her effective supply of labour would be defined as the notional supply, and his or her effective demand for any consumer good would be the quantity-constrained demand. In the case of the firm, its effective supply of output would be its notional supply and its effective demand for labour would be its quantity-constrained demand.

Second, effective demand failures are now possible because Walras's law does not extend to effective demands and supplies. It is possible for

$$\sum_i^n p_i E_i^e < 0$$

where E_i^e are excess effective demands. It is thus reasonable to imagine economies in states where some markets show excess supplies at positive prices and these are not balanced by excess demands on other markets. This means that there can be genuine unemployment. For instance, continuing with the above example, it is possible to envisage the following situation. Consumers' demand for goods is constrained by their inability to sell all the labour they supply, while firms do not employ more labour because the demand for goods is less than the amounts the firms are willing to supply. There is therefore an excess supply on both goods markets and labour markets simultaneously.

Third, economic agents' actions become dependent upon quantity variables in ways suggested by traditional Keynesian models. The level of aggregate consumption expenditure, for example, becomes dependent upon an income magnitude, which is determined by both quantities and prices. Moreover, a change in a quantity variable may alter others. The relaxation of a rationing constraint on labour sales will increase consumption expenditures, leading to a relaxation of quantity constraints on firms' sales, leading in turn to an increased demand for labour. In short, multiplier processes, which have no foundation in Walrasian theory, become possible. This also implies that the co-ordination of economic activities becomes a more complicated question to analyse because these activities can be interelated in more complex ways than is specified in Walrasian theory. Certainly the stability results of the latter are of little relevance since they pertain only to notional demands and supplies.

Fourth, from this perspective Keynesian economics appears more general than does Walrasian economics. The latter is seen as a special case of the former because it examines the particular case in which effective demands and supplies coincide with notional demands and supplies. This is certainly in line with Keynes's own view of the status of neoclassical economics.

Effective Demand Failures and Equilibrium

The ideas outlined in the preceding section can be traced back to the work of Clower (1965) and Leijonhuvud (1968), who derived them from Keynes (1936). They have been extended into new concepts of equilibrium by many economists, some of whom previously worked within the confines of Walrasian theory. These new concepts of equilibrium can be placed into two broad categories.

First, there has been the formulation of temporary equilibrium models, involving fixed prices and in which agents' maximisations take account of perceived quantity constraints in current and future periods. Equilibrium is defined as a situation where agents' maximisations generate constrained trades, i.e. effective demands and supplies, which are consistent. Various types of equilibria are possible and some of them involve genuinely unemployed resources.[15] The weakness of these models lies in treating prices as being exogenously fixed. The rationale for doing so is the belief that in modern capitalist economies quantity adjustments initially dominate price adjustments as the response to any change in effective demands and supplies. Consequently, such models do not imply that prices never change. The economy is pictured as moving through a sequence of quantity-constrained temporary equilibria, in each of which prices are given but between which they may change. If and how they change depend upon the determinants of prices. However, since the analysis concentrates upon a single period, prices are exogenously specified.

The second approach tries to overcome this weakness of fixed-price models. The essential idea is that agents who are rationed would willingly change prices if such changes were thought to yield a beneficial relaxation in the quantity constraints to which they are subject. Nevertheless, this willingness does not necessarily translate into price changes. Whether or not agents do change prices depends upon the 'conjectures' they hold as to how price changes will affect quantity constraints. For example, if an unemployed worker conjectures that a large reduction in his asking wage will only have a negligible impact upon the probability of gaining employment, this asking wage is unlikely to be reduced. The focus of attention is therefore upon what circumstances generate pessimistic conjectures, and the models, as so far developed, place emphasis upon incomplete information, imperfect competition and social conventions.[16] These can be such as to produce equilibria in which prices and quantity constraints are correctly forecast, so that economic processes terminate in states involving effective demand failures similar to those represented by fixed-price models but which continue over successive periods.

Conclusion

Concepts of effective demand and effective demand failures have been clearly established as theoretically viable. However, this does not imply that economic theorists will abandon neoclassical theory. The approach economists favour depends in part upon the pre-analytic vision they have of the phenomena which theory seeks to explain in a disciplined and orderly manner. We have touched on this elsewhere (see pp. 153—5) and it is also of relevance to theories of effective demand. An argument against the relevance of Keynesian models and favourable (at least in spirit) to neoclassical theory is in fact easily constructed from the way many neoclassical economists seem to perceive the nature of the market system. It could run as follows.

Market systems are essentially systems of voluntary trades. This means all parties to a set of trades must realise the maximal benefits possible, otherwise that set of trades will not be maintained. If any agent decides to form a new set of trades, he or she will need to signal other agents of this. The price system is one means of communication but it is not the only one. Market systems have evolved, and are still evolving, many systems of communication. In a situation Keynesians call effective demand failures, mutually beneficial trades obviously exist and it is equally obvious that it is in the interests of agents to locate them. Thus there can be a strong presumption that the Keynesian diagnosis is faulty and there can be an equally strong presumption in favour of an economics which formally incorporates, however inadequately, the adaptability and flexibility of market systems.[17]

Notes to Chapter 17

1. Non-satiation means that, no matter how large the consumption of any consumer, each consumer would prefer a larger consumption. This does not preclude any consumer from being satiated in the consumption of a particular commodity. It only implies that there is no consumer who is completely satisfied in the consumption of all commodities simultaneously.
2. See, for example, Dobb (1937), Schumpeter (1954), and Feinberg (1978).
3. Friedman (1969, p. 102).
4. Friedman (1969, p. 103).
5. See, for example, Friedman (1969, pp. 103–5; 1976, ch. 12).
6. See, for example, Friedman (1969).
7. See, for example, Lucas (1981, p. 48).
8. See, for example, Friedman (1976, ch. 12), Phelps (1970), and Lucas (1981).
9. Lucas (1981, pp. 4, 156, 242, 245).
10. See Phelps (1970) and Lucas (1981).
11. See also Hahn (1973; 1981), Arrow (1967; 1974), and Arrow and Hahn (1971).
12. See Hahn (1965; 1971; 1980a) and Tobin (1980, ch. 2).
13. See, for example, Rees (1970).
14. Robinson and Eatwell (1973, p. 48). See also Shackle (1967; 1972; 1974), Davidson (1972), and Coddington (1976).

15. Benassy (1975), Dreze (1975), Grandmont (1977), Malinvaud (1977; 1980), and Muellbauer and Portes (1978).
16. Negishi (1976; 1979), Hahn (1977; 1978; 1980a; 1980b), Akerloff (1979), and Buiter (1980).
17. These sentiments seem to be particularly pronounced in the work of Friedman. See Friedman (1962) and (1980).

18
Effective Demand and Profit in the Short Period

The Short Period

Effective demand theory has devoted very limited attention to the analysis of profit. It has been more concerned with establishing the coherence of its key concepts and utilising them to tackle employment problems. Nevertheless, the basic implications which variations in the level of effective demand have for total profits are easily deduced, as we have already seen in Chapter 16. These can be extended somewhat by using the work of Robinson.[1] She has very specific views concerning both the limitations of neoclassical economics and the nature of Keynesian theory. However, the models of profit determination which she has developed can be formulated sufficiently broadly as to accommodate alternative perspectives on both these matters.[2]

In this chapter we consider a typical Robinsonian model of the determinants of profit in short-period equilibria. These are particular types of Keynesian equilibria. Their defining quality is consideration of periods sufficiently short to preclude changes in productive capacity. Net investment may be positive but it is in the form of investment expenditures which will only change productive capacities at future dates beyond the period of analysis. However, outputs and employment can vary depending upon the utilisation of the given productive capacity induced by varying levels of effective demand.

Robinson considers three forces to be of primary importance for understanding profits in the short period:

1. *Capitalists' expenditure decisions*, or more generally the
   rate of aggregate investment and the pattern of savings
   behaviour exhibited by various types of agent.
2. *The pricing policy of firms*. This is usually conceptualised
   in terms of the 'degree of monopoly', a Kaleckian concept
   summarising the state of competition.[3] Here this is represented in terms of the 'mark-ups' on variable costs which
   firms use to determine their prices.
3. *The level of money wages prevailing*. Robinson considers
   the main factor lying behind this to be the relative 'bargaining strengths' of capitalists and workers.

We now consider how these three forces affect the level of
profits in short-period equilibria of a very simple economy.

Profits in Short-Period Keynesian Equilibria[4]

Let us assume an economy where the following assumptions
hold:

1. It is comprised of only two classes, capitalists and workers,
   which are mutually exclusive groups.
2. There are only two productive sectors, a capital-goods
   and a consumption-goods sector, each of which produces
   homogeneous outputs from a given productive capacity
   and is composed of identical firms.
3. The prevailing money wage is predetermined and there
   are constant unit wage costs up to capacity output in each
   sector.
4. Aggregate workers' saving is zero and any net investment
   (I) and/or capitalists' consumption expenditure (C_C) are
   exogenously determined.
5. Wages form the only variable cost of production and in
   each sector firms price by adding the same mark-up to
   their constant unit wage costs.

It follows from these assumptions that, in any equilibrium,

the flow of money demand for consumption goods is equal to the wages bill (W) plus capitalist consumption (C_C). The expenditure by workers engaged in producing consumption goods provides revenue for the firms in the consumption sector that exactly covers the wage bill in that sector. Profits in the consumption-goods sector are therefore equal to the wages bill of the investment sector plus the value of capitalist consumption. Profits in the capital-goods sector are equal to the value of investment minus the wages bill of workers engaged in producing the investment. Thus total profits are equal to $I + C_C$. In other words, the distributional relations uncovered above (pp. 160–3) continue to hold. We now proceed to compare various equilibria.

First, assume two equilibria with the same money value of investment and capitalist consumption, the same money wage prevailing, both with underutilisation of capacity but with firms in the different equilibria charging different mark-ups. The level of employment, output and money income is lower in the equilibrium with the higher mark-up. This is because a given total profit (equal to $I + C_C$) is made from a smaller output when profit per unit of output is greater. The pricing policy adopted, as reflected in the size of the mark-up, determines the share of profits in money income, though it does not affect the absolute amount of profits. The share of profits in income is determined by the ratio of investment plus capitalist consumption to money income, with the money income associated with the given $I + C_C$ being determined by the mark-up. Furthermore, given the money wage, the real wage is lower, the higher is the mark-up, so that both the income share of wages and the real wage are inversely associated with the size of the mark-up or the 'degree of monopoly'.

Now compare two equilibria with the same mark-up, the same value of capitalist consumption and the same money wage, but with different values of investment. The equilibrium with the higher investment has the higher employment and income. The higher profit associated with the higher investment must be gathered from higher production. The share of profits in income, and therefore the share of wages, is the same in both equilibria, as is the real wage. The same results as these follow if we compare two equilibria with the same mark-up, the same value of investment and money wage but with different values of capitalist consumption.

Another comparison we can make is between two equilibria, each with the same mark-up and the same value of investment and capitalist consumption, but with different money wage rates prevailing. The equilibrium with the higher money wage has the lower employment and output but in each equilibrium there is the same value of profits, the same profit and wage shares in income, and the same real wage. Investment and capitalist consumption in money terms are the same, so the equilibrium with the higher money wage produces less output as more absolute profit is made on the production of any commodity bundle involving the same employment. However, the same mark-up ensures the same shares of profit and wages in income, while the same value of investment and capitalist consumption ensures the same money profit. The price level in the equilibrium with the higher wage is higher in the same proportion, so the real wage is the same.

In comparing two equilibria with the same investment and capitalist consumption, with prices the same absolute amount above unit wage costs, but with different money wage rates, we obtain different results. The two equilibria have the same employment and output, and that with the higher money wage has a lower share of profit in income and therefore a higher wage share but it has the same value of profits. This is because the same profit (equal to investment plus capitalist consumption) is gathered by the same profit margin on each unit of output. Therefore, the same output and employment is needed to ensure the same absolute profits. Prices are higher in the equilibrium with the higher wage but not proportionately so in relation to the higher money wage. Thus there is a higher money income with the share of profits less, and the wage share and real wage greater. This can be taken to indicate a role for 'bargaining power'. If workers' organisations are sufficiently powerful to raise the money wage in one equilibrium but competition between firms is such that the mark-up is squeezed so that it is the same absolute amount above unit wage costs, then output and employment are the same but the real wage, the wage share and money income are higher. Prices are also higher but not in proportion to money wages.

Conclusion

In the simple model considered above, short-period profits are governed by only three influences: capitalists' expenditures, firms' pricing policies, and the level of the money wage. However, some other factors could be easily brought in and the model made more complex. Workers' saving, government expenditures, taxation and international trade would be the most obvious extensions suggested by the Keynesian perspective.[5]

The model was also formulated rather sparsely. Although to some this would represent a distinct advantage and certainly nothing to quibble about, economists trained in neoclassical theory would undoubtedly favour a choice-theoretic rationale for the assumptions employed. This is particularly so with regard to firms' pricing policies and the determinants of the money wage. These pose obvious problems for anyone who looks at this model through neoclassical eyes since they relate to prices, variables which neoclassical economists invariable regard as endogenous.

It should also be stressed that the results presented relate to comparisons of equilibria, not to the effects which a change will have on an economy in equilibrium. Of course, the motivation for undertaking such comparisons is to gain an insight into changes, but (as we have noted in another context on p. 84) conclusions drawn from comparisons need to be interpreted carefully. This has been continually emphasised by Robinson.[6] The disruption of any established equilibrium can change agents' expectations and actions in various ways depending on their previous experiences. Consequently, once out of equilibrium, the direction which the economy will take is not obvious. This matter has to be investigated separately from the question of what determines equilibrium magnitudes (see also pp. 190–1).

Furthermore, in the short-period model of this chapter, no mention was made of rates of profit. This was deliberate. A rate of profit is a ratio of profits to a capital value, and capital values are dependent upon anticipated future profits. In Walrasian intertemporal equilibria and rational expectations equilibria there is no problem in incorporating this because future profits are correctly anticipated. Apart from these cases, however, expectations may go astray so that any rate of profit defined on the basis of these expectations has no basis in reality. They are, literally speaking, figments of the imagination. However, just as in the case of neoclassical theory, we can overcome this by considering rational expectations equilibria. Indeed, Robinson has incorporated the three determining influences of short-period equilibrium profits into models applicable to the long period. We consider this in the following chapter.

Notes to Chapter 18

1. Robinson, (1956; 1960a; 1960b; 1962; 1965; 1971; 1973; 1978).
2. Robinson (1960b, p. 87). See also Howard (1979, p. 162).
3. Kalecki (1939; 1954).
4. This section draws heavily upon Howard (1979, pp. 143–7).
5. See, for example, Kregel (1973).
6. See, for example, Robinson (1975; 1978, p. vix).

19
Effective Demand and Profit in the Long Period

The Long Period

In this chapter the simple model specified in the previous chapter will be extended so as to allow analysis of 'long-period' relationships. The term 'long period' in this context refers to periods in which the productive capacity of the economy can change, or, put alternatively, to a sequence of 'short periods'.

In general, such a sequence is difficult to analyse unless agents' expectations turn out to be correct. If they become incorrect at any stage, assumptions have to be specified as to how agents revise the methods by which they form expectations and upon which their actions depend. Neither economists nor other social scientists know very much about this matter. Consequently, Keynesian theorists, like their neoclassical counterparts, have often assumed a sequence of short-period equilibria in which expectations are rational.[1] Such a sequence can be meaningful called a 'long-period equilibrium'.

Robinson has taken the view that these equilibria are only feasible in conditions of steady-state growth, in which the outputs of produced commodities all increase at the same constant rate, and where prices are stationary or change in a very simple manner. Only in this situation is it thought likely that experiences of agents will be clear and tranquil enough to generate rational expectations.[2]

The rational expectations of the steady-state equilibria, which we consider in the following section, are best interpreted in a stochastic manner (as outlined on pp. 166–7). There is no analytical requirement to do so, but it does allow a more sensible interpretation of the model. (For example, Robinson usually envisages firms' net investments to be positive, while simultaneously recognising that they retain underutilised productive capacity in normal circumstances. Unless the economy were subject to random distrubances this would make little sense.)

Profits in Long-Period Equilibria[3]

Let us add the following assumptions to those specified on page 179 of the previous chapter.

1. Each sector of the economy has a technology comprising a set of constant returns to scale processes of production. The processes in operation will depend upon the real wage or rate of profit which prevails. But whatever these are, mark-ups in each sector are such that, at 'normal' capacity levels, the rate of profit is uniform.
2. Technical progress is occurring at a constant rate and is 'neutral' in the sense that labour productivity is rising at the same rate in both sectors. With a uniform money wage prevailing in each period, relative prices of outputs remain unchanged, and with a constant rate of profit and money prices, the money wage and real wage will be rising at a rate equal to that of technical progress.
3. The labour force is growing at a constant rate, and depending upon the rate of growth of outputs and technical progress, the unemployment rate may be changing. For simplicity it is considered here to be constant.[4]
4. Capitalists are carrying out net investments at a constant rate and have a constant savings propensity (s_C).

From the assumptions we have made we can deduce a great deal about the distributional relations that must hold. The determinants of aggregate profits in any period are the same as those in the previous models. Thus profits are equal in value to investment and capitalist consumption. However, since capitalist consumption is now a function of current profits, this may be reformulated as $P = I + (1 - s_C)P$, which implies that $P = I/s_C$. Alternatively, we may deduce this result directly from the condition that investment equals saving, which means $I = s_C P$, again implying $P = I/s_C$.

The rate of profit on capital was not considered in the short-period models because it had little economic meaning (see above, p. 182). Here it does have clear meaning and, as we shall see, it determines the choice of technique the economy operates with, which in turn influences distributional shares in income. We can easily determine its magnitude. Reformulating the equilibrium condition as $I/K = S/K$, where K is the capital stock of the economy, and S is savings, $S = s_C P$, $r = P/K$, so $r = I/K/s_C$. The rate of profit determines the real wage, given technology (see above, pp. 43–5),[5] and since the rate of profit is constant the real wage must increase at a rate equal to the rate of technical progress. In any period a uniform money wage prevails, and this, in conjunction with technology and the rate of profit, determines money prices in that period. If money prices stay constant over time, the money wage must rise at the same rate as technical progress is occurring.

With a constant rate of unemployment and the labour force growing steadily, the total wages bill grows at the rate equal to the sum of the rates of growth of labour and technical progress. These factors of technical progress and labour growth are raising real and money income by the same magnitude. Thus the share of wages in income is constant. Consequently the share of profits is constant. Furthermore, since $S = s_C P$ and P/Y is constant, savings must grow at the same rate as income. This means that investment must grow at this rate also and that the ratio I/Y is a constant. We know that I/K (the rate of accumulation) is a constant, by assumption, which ensures that K/Y is therefore constant, so capital grows at the same rate as income. It follows that I/K must be equal to the sum of the rates of growth of labour and technical progress. If we denote this by the symbol g, we can write the rate of profit equation as $r = g/s_C$. Following Pasinetti (1974) we call this the *Cambridge equation*.

Now we proceed to examine different equilibria using the

same method of comparisons as that adopted in the exposition of the short-period theory.

Consider two equilibria, one with a higher mark-up in both sectors compared with the other but both with the same labour force, technology, rate of growth of labour, rate of technical progress, money wage and savings propensities. The rate of profit (equal to g/s_C) is independent of the pricing policy of firms, but the real wage is not. The prices of consumption goods are higher in the equilibrium with the higher mark-up, while by assumption the money wage is not. The only way these relationships can occur is for the equilibrium with the higher mark-ups to be associated with a lower level of capacity utilisation and thus a higher value of K/Y for the economy as a whole.

Now consider two equilibria, one with a higher rate of labour growth than the other and compare them at points where they both have the same labour force, set of technological processes, rate of technical progress, savings propensities and money wage. The rate of profit $(= (I/K)/s_C = g/s_C)$ will be higher in the equilibrium with the higher rate of labour growth. Associated with this higher rate of profit will be a lower real wage. Prices of consumption goods will be higher, reflecting the increased investment needs, and the money wage is, by assumption, the same. An almost similar situation arises if the two equilibria have different rates of technical progress, assuming the same rate of labour growth, labour force, set of technological processes, savings propensities and money wage. Again, the rate of profit will be higher and the real wage lower in the equilibrium experiencing the faster growth. However, the effect of differences in rates of labour growth and technical progress are not exactly the same. In the case of labour-growth differences the rate of increase of the real wage is the same in both equilibria but in the case of differences in rates of technical progress the real wage grows faster in the faster-growing equilibrium. Thus technical progress may be said to benefit the workers over time in a way that increases in numbers does not.

Finally, we can compare equilibria with different saving propensities but with the same rates of labour growth, technical progress, labour force, set of technological blue-prints and money wage. The equilibrium with the higher capitalists' savings propensity must have the lower rate of profit and the higher real wage. The rate of growth is the same in both, but the equilibrium with the higher savings propensity will have lower capitalist consumption, thus allowing lower prices of consumption goods relative to the given money wage. In these circumstances it is easy to see that the workers are best off when the capitalists' saving propensity is at a maximum, equal to unity. In this case profits function solely to provide the necessary resources to carry out the required investment necessary to keep the economy in long-period equilibrium.

In order to deal with the effect the above differences have on the income shares of the two classes we must consider the choice of processes from the profile of technology. The only case above where this may not be true is the first, where we dealt with differences in mark-ups. Since these do not change the rate of profit, there may be no difference in the processes employed in the different equilibria.

In such a case we can directly say that the equilibrium with the higher mark-up, associated with which is a higher K/Y, has the higher share of profits in income, and therefore the lower wage share. In all other cases the rate of profit is different, and consequently so too will be the processes in operation. If we assume that a lower rate of profit is associated with a higher capital—labour ratio, then clearly nothing can be said about the effect which a lower rate of profit will have on relative income shares without some knowledge of the relative magnitudes of these differences.

So far no direct mention has been made of the 'bargaining power' of the workers, though the comparison of economies with different mark-ups could be couched in these terms — the economy with the lower mark-up experiencing the greater 'bargaining strength' of the workers.

As was the case in Chapter 18, the method by which these factors are shown to influence profits is the method of comparing equilibria rather than the analysis of processes of change.

The above indicates that the same forces at work determining distribution in the short period also operate in the long period. In the latter, however, there is the additional influence of technology: the spectrum of techniques and technological progress, and the growth of the labour force.

The analysis in both cases was carried out in terms of very simple models, though Keynesians have considered distribution in more complex cases. Various types of steady growth have been examined by Robinson,[6] who has also considered financial institutions and scarce natural resources.[7] Pasinetti (1962) has shown that allowing for workers' savings does not necessarily undermine the applicability of the 'Cambridge equation'. Moreover, Pasinetti (1974) has considered a model in which there are many groups of both capitalists and workers, each with a distinct savings propensity. Kaldor (1966) has adapted the models to allow for corporate economic behaviour, and others, like Kregel (1973), have brought in government economic activity and international trade.

Surplus Theory

The Cambridge equation, $r = g/s_C$, provides a means whereby modern surplus models may be completed. As we have seen in Chapters 5 and 8, these models exhibit one degree of freedom and are not closed until a distributional variable is set at a specific level. Consequently, if Sraffa's systems are considered to represent economies in steady growth, the rate of profit as determined by Keynesian models may be appended to them. In the simple model described in this chapter, this rate of profit is given by the Cambridge equation. Pasinetti comments upon this as follows:

> For more than a century now, since the time of Marx and Böhm-Bawerk, economic theorists have been debating whether the rate of profits is due to any 'productivity' of capital and whether capital can in any sense be said to be 'productive'. But new horizons have been opened. In the long run . . . the rate of profit is determined by the natural rate of growth divided by the capitalists' propensity to save, independently of any 'productivity' of capital (no matter how it may be defined) and indeed independently of anything else. The most surprising outcome of all is that

the long-run rate of profit is even independent of 'capital'! In the long run, capital itself becomes a variable; and it is capital that has to be adapted to an exogensouly determined rate of profit, not the other way round.

The theoretical foundations are seen at their clearest when the relations are stripped down to their essentials — i.e. in the purest case in which $s_C = 1$ and therefore . . . the rate of profit is determined, fundamentally, not by the 'quantity of capital', but by the rates of growth of labour and of the productivity of labour.[8]

In a related context, Pasinetti also states that 'The post-Keynesian theories of economic growth and income distribution can be directly grafted on to the Ricardian theoretical framework, as if nothing had happened in between.'[9]

The limitations of such a marriage have already been considered. The arguments presented in Chapter 15 can be easily rephrased in such a way that they retain their relevance in this context. Furthermore, the two approaches to profit theory contain conflicting elements, as has been noted in chapters 8, 14 and 15. The tension is not a logical one. Formally, there is nothing to query in using the rate of profit determined by Keynesian reasoning to close surplus models. The problem is that surplus theory is inherently long run, whereas Keynesianism suggests that concentrating analysis on the short period is the key to understanding economic phenomena. This appears to be Robinson's own view[10] and it is a view which emerges from the nature of Keynesian analysis rather than being imposed upon it.

Subjectivities, especially agents' expectations, are clearly central to the Keynesian vision of the world and this is naturally incorporated into the structure of Keynesian models. The reason this does not appear as central in the model presented in this chapter is because subjective expectations have been chosen in order to ensure that they are in accord with 'objective' results. It appears thereby that the ' "effective demand" principle is independent of other Keynesian concepts bearing the traces of marginalism and its subjectivist approach'.[11]

The rationale for constructing long-period Keynesian models, such as that considered in this chapter, is primarily counterfactual. They can be used to highlight just how fragile are long-period equilibria and thus allow an examination of the various types of disturbance to which real economies may be subject.[12] Once such disturbances do occur the focus must be that of short-period analysis, and subjectivities loom to the surface as of overriding importance in understanding how the forces of effective demand will work themselves out.

Notes to Chapter 19

1. However, generally speaking, Keynesians hold different views as to the empirical relevance of this assumption. Robinson, in particular, has continually emphasised its lack of realism. (See this book, pp. 190–1.)
2. See, for example, Robinson (1960b, pp. 128–9, 132–44).
3. This section draws heavily upon Howard (1979, pp. 151–4).
4. Robinson delineates various types of steady state under the following nicknames. She calls a steady state where the desired rate of accumulation is equal to the 'maximum feasible rate' and where there is full employment of labour a 'golden age', 'intending thereby to indicate its mythical character' (Robinson, 1962, p. 52). The maximum feasible rate is the highest sustainable rate and is given by physical conditions in the model above; the relevant physical conditions are the growth rate of the labour force and the rate of increase in output per man due to technical progress. The maximum feasible rate is thus equal to the rate of growth of labour supply and technical progress. It is easy to see that the 'maximum feasible rate' is a maximum in a steady state. If capitalists desired to accumulate faster than this, the demand for labour will ultimately exceed the available supply. A 'limping golden age' is one where the desired rate of accumulation is such that there is unemployed labour. The 'limp' may be of various degrees of severity. Where there is a growing unemployment rate it is designated as a 'leaden age'. In contrast, where the desired rate of accumulation is such that it exceeds the maximum feasible rate, we have a 'restrained golden age'. In this situation, at full employment, the desired rate cannot be achieved and some check will have to come into operation (Robinson, 1962, pp. 54–5). Finally, we have a 'bastard golden age' where, although all the conditions for a form of golden-age growth exist, there is a limit on the rate of accumulation due to the real wage associated with the desired rate of accumulation being below what workers

will accept. In this situation various possibilities exist, some of which may place appropriate restraint on the desired rate of accumulation, while others may disrupt the steady state (Kahn, 1959).

5. The economy we are discussing can be represented technologically by relation (5.1), where $n = 2$ and the a_{ij} are considered unit input coefficients invariant to a change in scale.

6. See note 4 above.

7. Robinson (1956; 1973).

8. Pasinetti (1974, pp. 144–5).

9. Pasinetti (1974, p. 92).

10. See, for example, Robinson (1960b, p. 234; 1964, p. 79; 1971, p. 18; 1979), and Coddington (1976).

11. Garegnani (1978b, p. 75).

12. See, for example, Robinson (1960b, pp. 103–6, 120; 1971, pp. 75, 123; 1977, p. 1220). See also Harrod (1939) and Leijonhuvud (1981).

Part VI
REMAINING ISSUES

20
Some Loose Ends

Introduction

The preceeding chapters have been largely confined to explaining how various approaches visualise the elements considered essential to the understanding of profit, how these elements have been organised into formal theories and what results have been deduced. Consequently, the treatment has been rather narrow and somewhat dry. However, each of the approaches to profit which we have considered are associated with more general and informal ideas relevant to social analysis. In this final chapter some of these associations are highlighted and a number of issues which they raise are outlined.

Explaining Alternative Theories of Profit

The three approaches to the study of profit which formed the subject-matter of Parts II, III and V are each capable of formulating theories which are logically valid. Given their assumptions, their conclusions logically follow. This indicates that adherence to one approach in preference to the alternatives is based upon criteria other than that of internal coherence.

Positive economists, who are probably most strongly represented in neoclassical ranks, emphasise the importance of empirical relevance in the adoption of a particular theoretical approach.[1] However, it is difficult to explain the persistence of diverse schools in these terms. Those not in 'accordance with the evidence' could be expected to wither away. But this is not what appears to occur in the history of economic analysis. Instead, while some approaches suffer setbacks from time to time, they are reformulated and return to the fray. Thus, irrespective of how sensible positivism may be as a recommendation for choosing between alternative theories, it is distinctly limited in explaining the historical choices made by economists.

A related criterion of evaluation is an appeal to generality. Positivism may be inapplicable simply because the alternative theories fail to generate contrary testable propositions. In these circumstances it appears reasonable to adhere to that approach whose propositions are of wide applicability rather than those which can cover only 'special cases'.[2] The difficulty with this idea lies in specifying an acceptable concept of 'generality'. The problem here is that greater generality in conclusions does not come independently of other relevant matters. To get 'more general conclusions' compared with 'less general conclusions', assumptions have to be changed. This is only likely to be relatively uncontroversial within a particular approach because the change in this case is most likely to involve an unambiguous change to more general assumptions. Between approaches, the assumptions are different and are not capable of being described in terms of either more or less generality. Thus, while this criterion is of help in explaining the increasing dominance of Sraffian theory in the surplus tradition, or of Walrasian theory in neoclassical economics, it is relatively powerless to account for the different theoretical approaches to profit theory or in providing guidance in choosing between them.

Some surplus theorists, following Marx, have tended to take an altogether different tack by emphasising the ideological nature of economic theories, especially theories of profit.[3] From this perspective the adherence to a particular set of ideas stems from the social function which these ideas fulfil rather than their truth value. In the specific case of Marxian theory, these social functions are seen to be those of maintaining, or opposing, a system of surplus extraction, or exploitation. This argument, and others in the same vein, overcome the limitations inherent in the positions considered above. However, they do meet with other problems: namely, that of specifying the standards by which one linking of ideas to functions is judged superior, or valid, compared with another such linkage, and of explaining the mechanism by which such linkages occur. To associate a set of ideas with a set of functions can represent only a preliminary step. In addition, there is a need to spell out some criterion by which one such association can be considered more appropriate than another and, furthermore, an account of how the association of ideas with social functions came into existence. Without this, there is licence to construct all manner of plausible stories.

Social Order

A theory of profit is necessarily a theory of the economic systems in which profit arises. This means that a theory of profit is also a theory of capitalism. However, as considered in previous chapters, the theories of profit are theories of economic systems in only a very restricted sense. The light they throw is a very uneven one. They concentrate upon the relationship of profits to other economic phenomena in particular circumstances denoted by concepts of equilibrium. Two central issues, the problem of social order and economic development, are hardly touched upon. These are problems which one could reasonably expect a theory of profit to consider, or at least to be compatible with other theories that take them as central problems.

Social order, at first sight, appears to be particularly problematic for suprlus theory. In all forms the theories considered in Part II explained profit as arising from a surplus which is received by capitalists without the mediation of an exchange of equivalents. This is a principal reason why the term 'exploitation' is an apt one here. Naturally, therefore, the problem arises as to why a capitalist economy reproduces itself, of why agents in the system maintain the relationships which form the mechanism of surplus appropriation. However, this problem poses fewer difficulties for this kind of theory than initially appears to the case. The reason lies in the nature of the surplus approach itself, and in particular in fact that it does not focus upon decisions or choices of agents. As we have already noted in Chapter 2 (pp. 12–13) and Chapter 14 (pp. 143–4), agents are conceived as personnel fulfilling systemic functions and their actions are, therefore, determined by social properties so that concepts of choice and decision need not figure at all. This extreme materialist orientation fits in with the consideration raised in the previous section by focusing attention upon the role of ideas as ideologies.

The supply and demand theory of Part III and also a subjectivist interpretation of Keynesian theory, such as that given in Chapter 16, meets with greater difficulties on this score. These theories concentrate upon the activities of agents who are self-seeking, non-satiated and rational. This raises the problem of social order with a vengence. Why do those agents which historical experience shows do relatively poorly passively accept the institutional structure, or at least the distribution of income-generating assets? In these subjectivist approaches to economic theory there is orderly behaviour, in terms of which profit is explained, but the assumptions upon subjectivities throws into doubt such order.

Capitalist Development

Analysis of the 'laws of motion' of a capitalist system has been frequently associated with theories of profit. The reason for this is easy to appreciate. Production activities in such an economy are geared to profitability and it is from production activities that the chief sources of change appear to originate. On the other hand, these changes will react upon the conditions determining profits. Nevertheless, all the theories considered in the preceeding chapters carry no clear-cut implications regarding capitalist economic development.

The reason for this lies in the structure of these theories. In every case, profits are determined from a set of data and relations which are taken as being exogenous. These components have not proved easy to analyse, but are generally considered to be pivotal to the nature of development. For example, of central importance to all types of profit theory is the nature of technological input—output relations. However, theorists of all schools have not been able to specify the determinants of the speed and pattern of technical change sufficiently extensively to sustain a general theory of capitalist dynamics. More generally, the prospects of overcoming this limitation are perhaps worst for those theories which give prime attention to entrepreneurial expectations as a non-reducible element in causation

This means that the theories of profit we have considered exhibit a large degree of freedom regarding 'laws of motion'. It seems generally agreed that profit theory is essential to the understanding of these 'laws' and also that these 'laws' are essential for understanding the course of profits, but theories of profit as so far developed provide very little leverage on the matter.

Theoretical Orderliness

The last two sections reflect a set of implicit beliefs about the nature of appropriate theory construction. One such belief is that the causes of social and economic phenomena do exist and can be comprehended. This is uncontroversial, in the sense that it is a belief adhered to by all schools of economists. A second belief is more contentious. It is that causes are orderly or consistent and that theory should reflect this. In other words, theory construction is not simply an instrumental exercise devoted to formulating predictions. If the concern is practically limited in this sense, different problems can be tackled with different theories, each of whose assumptions need not be consistent. One simply picks out that amalgam of theories whose track records are most predictively accurate. On the other hand, if the aim is to construct theory which goes beyond this, assumptions have to be made which allow explanation of other phenomena associated with the specific problem at hand. Thus, for example, from this perspective a theory of profit whose assumptions brought into question the existence of the social context in which profit arises can be considered open to criticism irrespective of its internal logical coherence and predictive capabilities.

Economists and the Defence of Profits

Just as a theory of profit involves a theory of the economic organisation in which profit arises, so, too, a defence of profit which seeks to be taken seriously cannot be formulated in a social vacuum. This has not always been recognised by economists. For example, the concept of 'abstinence', developed by Senior (1836), was frequently used to rationalise the receipt of property income in the abstract. It was argued that since the maintenance of property entailed an abstention from consumption on the part of the owner, the income derived from such property could be regarded as a compensation for this psychic cost. A similar type of defence is provided by the productivity theories of capital, as they were developed in the mid-nineteenth century by Longfield and others. In this case it was maintained that a physical productivity underlay the receipt of profit by capitalists and, therefore, profit represented a return to a productive input, capital, in just the same way as wages represented a return to labour. Neither of these arguments has much force because they both implicitly assume relations of production involving private property and, more particularly, capitalist relations of production. If these are accepted as legitimate, it is redundant to defend their consequences.

However, economists have marshalled more sophisticated arguments in the defence of profits. They coalesce into two strands, one focusing upon freedom, the other on efficiency.

The first is represented by various philosophies of liberalism. The leading exponents of these doctrines frequently have been, and remain, economists.[4] The central idea is not a complicated one. It is held that human nature is so structured as to desire freedom, where this means an absence of constraints upon action. Obviously, social order requires that this not be absolute, but it is maintained by liberals that the limitations stemming from this requirement need only be negligible. And when freedom is extended to its practical limits, individuals' activities will generate private property, exchange, markets and profits. In this sense it may be said that *laissez-faire* capitalist is a natural order.

Although this argument does not rely upon any utilitarian

notion, it has nevertheless frequently been buttressed with arguments pertaining to the efficiency of a capitalist economic organisation. The most powerful strand is eloquently stated by Marx in the *Manifesto of the Communist Party*:

> The bourgeoisie, during its rule of scarce one hundred years, has created more massive and more colossal product-ive forces than have all preceding generations together. Subjection of Nature's forces to man, machinery, application of chemistry to industry and agriculture, steam-navigation, railways, electric telegraphs, clearing of whole continents for cultivation, canalisation of rivers, whole populations conjured out of the ground — what earlier century had even a presentiment that such productive forces slumbered in the lap of social labour?[5]

Schumpeter, in his *Capitalism, Socialism and Democracy* (1942), sought to flesh out this statement. His treatment remains the most powerful argument for capitalism on grounds of efficiency.

Economists and the Critique of Capitalism

In the modern world the leading doctrines explicitly hostile to liberalism are various forms of conservatism and socialism. They have similarities, and a central one is their defence of 'community' against the dissolving power of market relation-ships. Again Marx provides an exposition of these sentiments, in the following passage taken from the *Manifesto*:

> The bourgeoisie, wherever it has got the upper hand, has put an end to all feudal, patriarchal, idyllic relations. It has pitilessly torn asunder the motley feudal ties that bound man to his 'natural superiors', and has left remaining no other nexus between man and man than naked self-interest, than callous 'cash payment'. It has drowned the most heavenly ecstasies of religious fervour, of chivalrous enthus-iasms, of philistine sentimentalism, in the icy water of egotistical calculation. It has resolved personal worth into

exchange value, and in place of the numberless indefeasible chartered freedoms, has set up that single, unconscionable freedom — Free Trade.[6]

Marx's ethical critique of capitalism is in fact much deeper than this quotation suggests, and is of course radical rather than conservative in orientation. It is founded upon an alternative conception of human nature, and of human freedom, from that espoused by liberal theorists. For Marx, as for liberals, freedom represents a state of affairs conforming to human nature. The difference lies in the conception of 'humanity'. At its most abstract, Marx conceptualises this as an ability to engage in conscious transformative action in both the natural and social worlds: the capability of creating environments in conformity with historically developing human needs. Thus freedom is identified with conscious mastery of both nature and social relations. This would represent a condition in which all individuals are able fully to develop personal capabilities in both material and intellectual activities: in short, to determine consciously what they are and will become. Since an individual is not an island, such power is necessarily social and is only meaningful when society is unified as a community and not divided by competition or conflict as in capitalism.[7]

These philosophies, whether socialist or conservative, have rarely formed, however, the foundation of the critiques levelled by economists against an economic system based upon profits. Generally they have preferred a nitty-gritty, issue-specific, approach within an ill-defined framework of values. This is especially true of contemporary neoclassical economists. In this they have been instrumental in the intellectual process by which classical liberal ideas have become transformed into those of social democracy or 'modern' (reformist) liberalism. The two key concepts employed have been those of 'market failure' and 'equity'.

Market failure has indeed been the vehicle allowing a 'working relation' to be formed between neoclassical and Keynesian economists, for markets fail most obviously when they do not clear. The response by economists has generally been to favour macro 'management' of market forces, to manipulate expenditures in an attempt to stabilise economies around equilibria involving a balance of supplies and demands in the aggregate. Economic control has been reinforced by the theory of externalities, interactions which occur between agents which are not covered by market contracts (the classic example of which is pollution). When such externalities occur, it is easy to show that central management could, with sufficient information available, improve economic performance on the criteria of Paretian welfare economics. Currently, the analysis of various types of externality has developed into a large industry and its propositions are clearly out of tune with those of classical liberalism.

Equity considerations have further supported this tendency. Neoclassical economists, for the most part, have seen the main defect of capitalism to be the very large and persistent economic inequalities it has generated. Consequently, they have sought to formulate efficient methods of redistribution, implemented via government expenditures and taxation. Naturally, schemes pertaining to the redistribution of profits and other property incomes have figured prominently here.

The sentiments behind the mainstream of economic theory therefore favour a managed profit system, the instrument of management being placed upon the institutions of the state. This has been theoretically convenient. State institutions and policies have always been regarded as exogenous by subjectivist economic theory. Consequently, they could be treated as agencies of rational 'policy'. To what extent the nature of capitalist society will actually allow such a role has not been seriously considered.

Notes to Chapter 20

1. Friedman (1953) is one formulation of this stand. For a more general discussion see Ryan (1970), Keat and Urry (1975), Coddington (1972), and Blaug (1980).
2. See, for example, Schumpeter (1954), Koopmans (1957), Bliss (1975), and Steedman (1977).

3. See, for example, Marx and Engels (1845), Marx (1862a; 1862b; 1862c), Meek (1967), and Dobb (1973).
4. For example, Smith (1776), Mill (1859), Hayek (1944), and Friedman (1962).
5. Marx and Engels (1848, p. 113).
6. Marx and Engels (1848, p. 111). For an exposition of conservatism see Nisbet (1979) and Scruton (1980).
7. See, for example, Marx (1844).

References

Abraham-Frois, E. and Berrebi, E. (1979) *Theory of Values, Prices and Accumulation: A Mathematical Integration of Marx, Von Neumann and Sraffa*, Cambridge, Cambridge University Press.

Akerloff, G. A. (1979) 'The Case against Conservative Macroeconomics: An Inaugural Lecture', *Economica*, vol. 46, pp. 219—37.

Alchian, A. A. (1970) 'Information Costs, Pricing, and Resource Unemployment', in Phelps (1970), pp. 27—52.

Althusser, L. (1969) *For Marx*, Harmondsworth, Penguin.

Andrews, P. W. S. (1964) *On Competition in Economic Theory*, London, Macmillan.

Armstrong, P., Glyn, A. and Harrison, J. (1978) 'In Defence of Value: A Reply to Ian Steedman', *Capital and Class*, vol. 5, Summer, pp. 1—31.

Arrow, K. J. (1953) 'Le role des valeurs boursieres pour la repartition la meilleure des risques', in *International Colloquium of Econometrics*, Paris, Centre National de la Recherche Scientifique.

Arrow, K. J. (1967) 'Samuelson Collected', *Journal of Political Economy*, vol. 75, pp. 730—7.

Arrow, K. J. (1971a) 'The Firm in General Equilibrium Theory', in Marris and Wood (1971), pp. 68—110.

Arrow, K. J. (1971b) *Essays in the Theory of Risk Bearing*, Amsterdam, North-Holland.

Arrow, K. J. (1974) 'Limited Knowledge and Economic Analysis', *American Economic Review*, vol. 64, pp. 1—10.

Arrow, K. J. (1976) *The Viability and Equity of Capitalism*, Vancouver, University of British Columbia.

Arrow, K. J. (1978) 'The Future and Present in Economic Life', *Economic Inquiry*, vol. 16, pp. 157—69.

Arrow, K. J. and Hahn, F. H. (1971) *General Competitive Analysis*, Edinburgh, Oliver & Boyd.

Arrow, K. J. and Starrett, D. A. (1973) 'Cost — and Demand — Theoretical Approaches to the Theory of Price Determination', in Hicks and Weber (1973), pp. 129—48.

Artis, M. I. and Nobay, A. R. (eds) (1976) *Essays in Economic Analysis*, Cambridge, Cambridge University Press.

206   *References*

Aumann, R. J. (1964) 'Markets with a Continuum of Traders', *Econometrica*, vol. 32, pp. 39—50.

Beenstock, M. (1980) *A Neoclassical Analysis of Macroeconomic Policy*, Cambridge, Cambridge University Press.

Benassy, J. P. (1975) 'Neo-Keynesian Disequilibrium Theory in a Monetary Economy', *Review of Economic Studies*, vol. 42, pp. 503—24.

Bhaduri, A. (1969) 'On the Significance of Recent Controversies on Capital Theory: A Marxian View', *Economic Journal*, vol. 79, pp. 532—9.

Blaug, M. (1978) *Economic Theory in Retrospect*, 3rd edn, Cambridge, Cambridge University Press.

Blaug, M. (1980) *The Methodology of Economics*, Cambridge, Cambridge University Press.

Bliss, C. J. (1975) *Capital Theory and the Distribution of Income*, Amsterdam, North-Holland.

Böhm-Bawerk, E. von (1888) *The Positive Theory of Capital*, New York, Stechert (ed. W. Smart, 1891).

Bortkiewicz, L. von (1907) 'On the Correction of Marx's Fundamental Theoretical Construction in the Third Volume of "Capital" ', in Sweezy (1966).

Bottomore, T. and Nisbet, R. (eds) (1979) *A History of Sociological Analysis*, London, Heinemann.

Bradley, I. G. and Howard, M. C. (eds) (1982a) *Classical and Marxian Political Economy*, London, Macmillan.

Bradley, I. G. and Howard, M. C. (1982b) 'An Introduction to Classical and Marxian Political Economy', in Bradley and Howard (1982a), pp. 1—43.

Bradley, I. G. and Howard, M. C. (1982c) 'Piero Sraffa's "Production of Commodities by Means of Commodities" and the Rehabilitation of Classical and Marxian Political Economy', in Bradley and Howard (1982a), pp. 229—54.

Bronfenbrenner, M. (1960) 'A Reformulation of Naive Profit Theory', *Southern Economic Journal*, vol. 26, pp. 300—9.

Brown, M., Sato, K. and Zarembka, P. (eds) (1976) *Essays in Modern Capital Theory*, Amsterdam, North-Holland.

Buiter, W. H. (1980) 'The Macroeconomics of Dr. Pangloss: A Critical Survey of the New Classical Macroeconomics', *Economic Journal*, vol. 90, pp. 34—50.

Burmeister, E. (1974) 'Synthesizing the Neo-Austrian and Alternative Approaches to Capital Theory: A Survey', *Journal of Economic Literature*, vol. 12, pp. 413—56.

Champernowne, D. E. (1953) 'The Production Function and the Theory of Capital', *Review of Economic Studies*, vol. 21, pp. 112—35. Reprinted in Harcourt and Laing (1971), from which references are taken.

Chipman, T. S. (1965) 'The Nature and Meaning of Equilibrium in Economic Theory', in Townsend (1971), pp. 341—71.

Clark, J. B. (1894) 'The Genesis of Capital', *Yale Review*, vol. 2, pp. 302–15.

Clark, J. B. (1895) 'The Origin of Interest', *Quarterly Journal of Economics*, vol. 9, pp. 257–78.

Clark, J. B. (1899) *The Distribution of Wealth*, London, Macmillan.

Clower, R. W. (1965) 'The Keynesian Counter-Revolution: A Theoretical Appraisal', in Hahn and Brechling (1965), pp. 103–25.

Cobb, C. W. and Douglas, P. H. (1928) 'A Theory of Production', *American Economic Review*, vol. 18, pp. 139–65.

Coddington, A. (1972) 'Positive Economics', *Canadian Journal of Economics*, vol. 5, pp. 1–15.

Coddington, A. (1976) 'Keynesian Economics: The Search for First Principles', *Journal of Economic Literature*, vol. 14, pp. 1258–72.

Davidson, P. (1972) *Money and the Real World*, London, Macmillan.

Davis, R. M. (1952) 'The Current State of Profit Theory', *American Economic Review*, vol. 42, pp. 245–64.

Debreu, G. (1959) *Theory of Value*, New Haven, Conn., Yale University Press.

Dixit, A. (1977) 'The Accumulation of Capital Theory', *Oxford Economic Papers*, vol. 29, pp. 1–29.

Dmitriev, V. (1898) *Economic Essays on Value, Competition and Utility*, Cambridge, Cambridge University Press (trans. D. Fry, ed. D. M. Nuti, 1973).

Dobb, M. H. (1937) *Political Economy and Capitalism*, London, Routledge & Kegan Paul.

Dobb, M. H. (1973) *Theories of Value and Distribution Since Adam Smith*, Cambridge, Cambridge University Press.

Dougherty, C. R. S. (1972) 'On the Rate of Return and the Rate of Profit', *Economic Journal*, vol. 82, pp. 1324–50.

Dougherty, C. R. S. (1980) *Interest and Profit*, London, Methuen.

Douglas, P. H. (1948) 'Are There Laws of Production?', *American Economic Review*, vol. 38, pp. 1–41.

Dreze, J. (1975) 'Existence of an Exchange Equilibrium Under Price Rigidities', *International Economic Review*, vol. 16, pp. 301–20.

Eatwell, J. E. (1971) 'Growth, Profitability and Size: The Empirical Evidence', in Marris and Wood (1971), pp. 389–21.

Eatwell, J. E. (1973) 'Controversies in the Theory of Surplus Value: Old and New', *Science and Society*, vol. 38, pp. 281–303.

Eatwell, J. E. (1975) 'Mr. Sraffa's Standard Commodity and the Rate of Exploitation', *Quarterly Journal of Economics*, vol. 89, pp. 543–55.

Eatwell, J. E. (1976) 'Irving Fisher's "Rate of Return Over Cost" and the Rate of Profit in a Capitalistic Economy', in Brown, Sato and Zarembka (1976), pp. 77–96.

Eatwell, J. E. (1982) 'Competition', in Bradley and Howard (1982a), pp. 203–28.

Erlich, A. (1967) 'Notes on the Marxian Model of Capital Accumulation', *American Economic Review*, vol. 57, pp. 599–616.

208   *References*

Feinberg, R. M. (1978) 'The Forerunners of the Job Search Theory', *Economic Inquiry*, vol. 16, pp. 126–31.

Fellner, W. (ed.) (1967) *Ten Economic Studies in the Tradition of Irving Fisher*, New York, Wiley.

Fisher, I. (1907) *The Rate of Interest*, New York, Macmillan.

Fisher, I. (1930) *The Theory of Interest*, New York, Macmillan.

Flux, A. W. (1894), Review of Wicksteed (1894), *Economic Journal*, vol. 4, pp. 305–13.

Friedman, M. (1953) *Essays in Positive Economics*, Chicago, University of Chicago Press.

Friedman, M. (1962) *Capitalism and Freedom*, Chicago, University of Chicago Press.

Friedman, M. (1969) *The Optimum Quantity of Money*, London, Macmillan.

Friedman, M. (1976) *Price Theory*, 2nd edn, Chicago, Aldine.

Friedman, M. (1980) *Free to Choose*, New York, Harcourt Brace Jovanovich.

Gaitskell, H. T. N. (1936) 'Notes on the Period of Production, Part I', *Zeitschrift für Nationalöekonomie*, vol. 7, pp. 577–95.

Gaitskell, H. T. N. (1938) 'Notes on the Period of Production, Part II', *Zeitschrift für Nationalöekonomie*, vol. 9, pp. 215–44.

Garegnani, P. (1970a) 'Heterogeneous Capital, the Production Function and the Theory of Distribution', *Review of Economic Studies*, vol. 37, pp. 407–36.

Garegnani, P. (1970b) 'A Reply', *Review of Economic Studies*, vol. 37, p. 439.

Garegnani, P. (1973) 'Summary of the Final Discussion', in Mirrlees and Stern (1973).

Garegnani, P. (1976) 'On a Change in the Notion of Equilibrium in Recent Work on Value and Distribution: A Comment on Samuelson', in Brown, Sato and Zarembka (1976), pp. 25–45.

Garegnani, P. (1978a) 'Notes on Consumption, Investment and Effective Demand: I', *Cambridge Journal of Economics*, vol. 2, pp. 335–53.

Garegnani, P. (1978b) 'Sraffa's Revival of Marxist Economic Theory', *New Left Review*, no. 112, pp. 71–5.

Garegnani, P. (1979) 'Notes on Consumption, Investment and Effective Demand: II', *Cambridge Journal of Economics*, vol. 3, pp. 63–82.

Goldschmid, H. J., Mann, M. M. and Weston, J. F. (eds) (1974) *Industrial Concentration and New Learning*, Boston, Little, Brown.

Grandmont, J. M. (1977) 'Temporary General Equilibrium Theory', *Econometrica*, vol. 45, pp. 535–72.

Güsten, R. (1965) 'Bemerkungen zur Marxchen Theorie des Technischen Fortschrittes', *Jahrbücher für Nationalöekonomie*, vol. 178, pp. 109–21.

Hahn, F. H. (1947) 'A Note on Profit and Uncertainty', *Economica*, vol. 14, pp. 211–25.

Hahn, F. H. (1965) 'On Some Problems of Proving the Existence of an

Equilibrium in a Monetary Economy', in Hahn and Brechling (1965), pp. 126–35.

Hahn, F. H. (1971) 'Professor Friedman's Views on Money', *Economica*, vol. 38, pp. 61–80.

Hahn, F. H. (1973) *On the Notion of Equilibrium in Economics: An Inaugural Lecture*, Cambridge, Cambridge University Press.

Hahn, F. H. (1977) 'Keynesian Economics and General Equilibrium Theory: Reflections on Some Current Debates', in Harcourt (1977), pp. 25–40.

Hahn, F. H. (1978) 'On Non-Walrasian Equilibria', *Review of Economic Studies*, vol. 45, pp. 1–17.

Hahn, F. H. (1980a) 'Monetarism and Economic Theory', *Economica*, vol. 47, pp. 1–17.

Hahn, F. H. (1980b) 'Unemployment from a Theoretical Viewpoint', *Economica*, vol. 47, pp. 285–98.

Hahn, F. H. (1981) Review of Beenstock (1980), *Economic Journal*, vol. 91, pp. 1036–9.

Hahn, F. H. and Brechling, F. (eds) (1965) *The Theory of Interest Rates*, London, Macmillan.

Hahn, F. H. and Matthews, R. C. O. (1964) 'The Theory of Economic Growth: A Survey', *Economic Journal*, vol. 74, pp. 779–902.

Harcourt, G. C. (1972) *Some Cambridge Controversies in the Theory of Capital*, Cambridge, Cambridge University Press.

Harcourt, G. C. (ed.) (1977) *The Microeconomic Foundations of Macroeconomics*, Cambridge, Macmillan.

Harcourt, G. C. (1982) 'The Sraffian Contribution: An Evaluation', in Bradley and Howard (1982a), pp. 255–75.

Harcourt, G. C. and Laing, N. F. (eds) (1971) *Capital and Growth: Selected Readings*, Harmondsworth, Penguin.

Harris, D. J. (1978) *Capital Accumulation and Income Distribution*, Stanford, Stanford University Press.

Harrod, R. F. (1939) 'An Essay in Dynamic Theory', *Economic Journal*, vol. 49, pp. 14–33.

Hayek, F. A. von (1931) *Prices and Production*, New York, Kelly (1967).

Hayek, F. A. von (1939) *Profits, Interest and Investment*, London, Routledge.

Hayek, F. A. von (1941) *The Pure Theory of Capital*, Chicago, University of Chicago Press.

Hayek, F. A. von (1944) *The Road to Serfdom*, Chicago, University of Chicago Press.

Hicks, J. R. (1931) 'The Theory of Uncertainty and Profit', *Economica*, vol. 21, pp. 170–89.

Hicks, J. R. (1932) *The Theory of Wages*, London, Macmillan.

Hicks, J. R. (1939) *Value and Capital*, Oxford, Oxford University Press (2nd edn, 1946).

Hicks, J. R. (1963) 'Commentary' on *The Theory of Wages*, in Hicks (1932, 1963 edn), pp. 305–372.

Hicks, J. R. (1970) 'A Neo-Austrian Growth Theory', *Economic Journal*, vol. 80, pp. 257—81.

Hicks, J. R. (1973a) *Capital and Time: A Neo-Austrian Theory*, Oxford, Oxford University Press.

Hicks, J. R. (1973b) 'The Austrian Theory of Capital and its Rebirth in Modern Economics', in Hicks and Weber (1973), pp. 190—206.

Hicks, J. R. (1975) 'Revival of Political Economy: The Old and the New', *Economic Record*, vol. 51, pp. 365—7.

Hicks, J. R. (1976) 'Some Questions of Time in Economics', in Tang, Westfield and Worley (1976), pp. 135—51.

Hicks, J. R. and Weber, W. (eds) (1973), *Carl Menger and the Austrian School of Economics*, Oxford, Oxford University Press.

Hirshleifer, J. (1970) *Investment, Interest and Capital*, Englewood Cliffs, N.J., Prentice-Hall.

Howard, M. C. (1979) *Modern Theories of Income Distribution*, London, Macmillan.

Howard, M. C. (1980) 'Austrian Capital Theory: An Evaluation in Terms of Piero Sraffa's "Production of Commodities by Means of Commodities" ', *Metroeconomica*, vol. 32, pp. 1—23.

Howard, M. C. (1981) 'Ricardo's Analysis of Profit: An Evaluation in Terms of Piero Sraffa's "Production of Commodities by Means of Commodities" ', *Metroeconomica*, vol. 33.

Howard, M. C. and King, J. E. (1975) *The Political Economy of Marx*, London, Longman.

Howard, M. C. and King, J. E. (eds) (1976) *The Economics of Marx: Selected Readings of Exposition and Criticism*, Harmondsworth, Penguin.

Hunt, E. K. and Schwartz, J. G. (eds) (1972) *A Critique of Economic Theory: Selected Readings*, Harmondsworth, Penguin.

Jevons, W. S. (1871) *The Theory of Political Economy*, Harmondsworth, Penguin (1970).

Johnson, H. G. (1966) 'The Neo-Classical One Sector Growth Model: A Geometrical Exposition and Extension to a Monetary Economy', *Economica*, vol. 33, pp. 265—87.

Johnson, H. G. (1973) *The Theory of Income Distribution*, London, Gray Mills.

Kahn, R. F. (1959) 'Exercises in the Analysis of Growth', *Oxford Economic Papers*, vol. 11, pp. 143—56.

Kaldor, N. (1937) 'Annual Survey of Economic Theory: The Recent Controversy on the Theory of Capital', *Econometrica*, vol. 5, pp. 201—33.

Kaldor, N. (1956) 'Alternative Theories of Distribution', *Review of Economic Studies*, vol. 23, pp. 83—100. Reprinted in McCormick and Smith (1968), pp. 349—79, from which references are taken.

Kaldor, N. (1966) 'Marginal Productivity and the Macro Economic Theories of Distribution', *Review of Economic Studies*, vol. 33, pp. 309—19.

Kalecki, M. (1939) *Essays in the Theory of Economic Fluctuations*, London, Allen & Unwin.

Kalecki, M. (1954) *Theory of Economic Dynamics*, London, Allen & Unwin.

Kalecki, M. (1971) *Selected Essays on the Dynamics of the Capitalist Economy 1933–1970*, Cambridge, Cambridge University Press.

Keat, R. N. and Urry, J. R. (1975) *Social Theory as Science*, London, Routledge & Kegan Paul.

Keynes, J. M. (1931) *A Treatise on Money*, London, Macmillan.

Keynes, J. M. (1936) *The General Theory of Employment, Interest and Money*, London, Macmillan.

Keynes, J. M. (1937) 'The General Theory of Employment', *Quarterly Journal of Economics*, vol. 51, pp. 209–23.

King, J. E. (1982) 'Value and Exploitation: Some Recent Debates', in Bradley and Howard (1982a), pp. 157–87.

Klundert, Th. van de and Schaik, A. van (1974) 'Durable Capital and Economic Growth', *De Economist*, vol. 122, pp. 206–24.

Knight, F. H. (1921) *Risk, Uncertainty and Profit*, Boston, Houghton Mifflin.

Knight, F. H. (1933) 'Capitalistic Production, Time and the Rate of Return', in *Essays in Honour of Gustav Cassel*, London, Allen & Unwin, pp. 327–43.

Knight, F. H. (1934) 'Profit', *Encyclopedia of the Social Sciences*, vol. 12, New York, Macmillan, pp. 480–6.

Knight, F. H. (1936) 'Capital and Interest', *Encyclopaedia Britannica*, vol. 4, pp. 779–801.

Koopmans, T. C. (1957) *Three Essays on the State of Economic Science*, New York, McGraw-Hill.

Koutsoyiannis, A. (1979) *Modern Microeconomics*, London, Macmillan.

Kregel, J. (1973) *The Reconstruction of Political Economy*, London, Macmillan.

Kuenne, R. E. (1971) *Eugen von Böhm-Bawerk*, New York, Columbia University Press.

Kurz, H. D. (1979) 'Sraffa After Marx', *Australian Economic Papers*, vol. 18, pp. 32–70.

Laibman, D. (1973) 'Values and Prices of Production: The Political Economy of the Transformation Problem', *Science and Society*, vol. 37, pp. 404–36.

Lamberton, D. M. (1965) *The Theory of Profit*, Oxford, Blackwell.

Lange, O. (1936) 'The Place of Interest in the Theory of Production', *Review of Economic Studies*, vol. 3, pp. 159–92.

Leijonhuvud, A. (1968) *On Keynesian Economics and the Economics of Keynes*, Oxford, Oxford University Press.

Leijonhuvud, A. (1981) *Information and Coordination*, Oxford, Oxford University Press.

Lindahl, E. (ed.) (1958) *Knut Wicksell: Selected Papers on Economic Theory*, London, Allen & Unwin.

Lucas, R. E. (1981) *Studies in Business Cycle Theory*, Cambridge, Mass., MIT Press.

Lukes, S. (1968) 'Methodological Individualism Reconsidered', *British Journal of Sociology*, vol. 19, pp. 119–29.

McConnell, C. R. and Pope, W. H. (1981) *Economics*, New York, McGraw-Hill.

McCormick, B. and Smith, E. O. (eds) (1968) *The Labour Market*, Harmondsworth, Penguin.

Malinvaud, E. (1953) 'Capital Accumulation and Efficient Allocation of Resources', *Econometrica*, vol. 21, pp. 233–68.

Malinvaud, E. (1977) *The Theory of Unemployment Reconsidered*, Oxford, Blackwell.

Malinvaud, E. (1980) *Profitability and Unemployment*, Cambridge, Cambridge University Press.

Malthus, T. R. (1803) *An Essay on the Principle of Population*, Harmondsworth, Penguin (1970).

Manara, C. F. (1968) 'Sraffa's Model for Joint Production of Commodities by Means of Commodities', in Pasinetti (1980a), pp. 1–15.

Marshall, A. (1890) *Principles of Economics*, London, Macmillan.

Marris, R. and Wood, A. (eds) (1971) *The Corporate Economy*, Cambridge, Mass., Harvard University Press.

Marx, K. (1844) *Economic and Philosophic Manuscripts of 1844*, London, Lawrence & Wishart (1970).

Marx, K. (1857) *Grundrisse*, Harmondsworth, Penguin (1973).

Marx, K. (1862a) *Theories of Surplus-Value: Part I*, London, Lawrence & Wishart (1969).

Marx, K. (1862b) *Theories of Surplus-Value: Part II*, London, Lawrence & Wishart (1972).

Marx, K. (1862c) *Theories of Surplus-Value: Part III*, London, Lawrence & Wishart (1972).

Marx, K. (1867) *Capital: Volume I*, London, Lawrence & Wishart (1970).

Marx, K. (1885) *Capital: Volume II*, London, Lawrence & Wishart (1970).

Marx, K. (1894) *Capital: Volume III*, London, Lawrence & Wishart (1972).

Marx, K. and Engels, F. (1845) *The German Ideology*, London, Lawrence & Wishart (1970).

Marx, K. and Engels, F. (1848) *Manifesto of the Communist Party*, in *Selected Works*, vol. I, Moscow, Progress Publishers (1969), pp. 98–137.

Meade, J. E. (1961) *A Neoclassical Theory of Economic Growth*, London, Allen & Unwin.

Medio, A. (1972) 'Profits and Surplus-Value: Appearance and Reality in Capitalist Production', in Hunt and Schwartz (1972), pp. 312–46.

Meek, R. L. (ed.) (1962) *The Economics of Physiocracy*, London, Allen & Unwin.

Meek, R. L. (1967) *Economics and Ideology and Other Essays*, London, Chapman & Hall.

Meek, R. L. (1977) *Smith, Marx and After*, London, Chapman & Hall.

Metzler, L. A. (1950) 'The Rate of Interest and the Marginal Product of Capital', *Journal of Political Economy*, vol. 58, pp. 289–306.

Mill, J. S. (1859) *On Liberty*, London, Dent (1910).

Milgate, M. (1979) 'On the Origin of the Notion of "Intertemporal Equilibrium" ', *Economica*, vol. 46, pp. 1–10.

Mirrlees, J. A. and Stern, N. H. (eds) (1973) *Models of Economic Growth*, London, Macmillan.

Morishima, M. (1973) *Marx's Economics*, Cambridge, Cambridge University Press.

Morishima, M. (1974) 'Marx in the Light of Modern Economic Theory', *Econometrica*, vol. 42, pp. 611–23.

Morishima, M. and Catephores, G. (1978) *Value, Exploitation and Growth*, New York, McGraw-Hill.

Muellbaur, J. and Portes, R. (1978) 'Macroeconomic Models with Quantity Rationing', *Economic Journal*, vol. 88, pp. 788–821.

Naslund, B. and Sellstedt, O. (1978) *Neo-Ricardian Theory*, Berlin, Springer Verlag.

Negishi, T. (1961) 'Monopolistic Competition and General Equilibrium', *Review of Economic Studies*, vol. 28, pp. 196–201.

Negishi, T. (1962) 'The Stability of the Competitive Equilibrium: A Survey Article', *Econometrica*, vol. 30, pp. 635–70.

Negishi, T. (1976) 'Unemployment, Inflation and the Micro Foundations of Macroeconomics', in Artis and Nobay (1976), pp. 33–49.

Negishi, T. (1979) *Microeconomic Foundations of Keynesian Macroeconomics*, Amsterdam, North-Holland.

Nell, E. (1980) *Growth, Profits and Property*, Cambridge, Cambridge University Press.

Neumann, J. von (1937) 'A Model of General Economic Equilibrium', *Review of Economic Studies*, vol. 13 (1945), pp. 1–9.

Nisbet, R. (1979) 'Conservatism', in Bottomore and Nisbet (1979), pp. 80–117.

Nuti, D. M. (1970) 'Capitalism, Socialism and Steady Growth', *Economic Journal*, vol. 80, pp. 32–54.

Parkin, M. and Nobay, A. (eds) (1975) *Current Economic Problems*, Cambridge, Cambridge University Press.

Pasinetti, L. L. (1962) 'Rate of Profit and Income Distribution in Relation to the Rate of Economic Growth', *Review of Economic Studies*, vol. 29, pp. 267–79.

Pasinetti, L. L. (1966) 'Changes in the Rate of Profit and Switches in Technique', *Quarterly Journal of Economics*, vol. 80, pp. 503–17.

Pasinetti, L. L. (1969) 'Switches in Technique and the "Rate of Return" in Capital Theory', *Economic Journal*, vol. 79, pp. 508–31. Reprinted in Harcourt and Laing (1971), from which references are taken.

Pasinetti, L. L. (1974) *Growth and Income Distribution*, Cambridge, Cambridge University Press.

Pasinetti, L. L. (1977a) *Lectures on the Theory of Production*, London, Macmillan.

Pasinetti, L. L. (1977b) 'On "Non-Substitution" in Production Models', *Cambridge Journal of Economics*, vol. 1, pp. 389–94.

Pasinetti, L. L. (ed.) (1980a) *Essays on the Theory of Joint Production*, London, Macmillan.

Pasinetti, L. L. (1980b) 'A Note on Basics, Non-Basics and Joint Production', in Pasinetti (1980a), pp. 51–4.

Pauly, M. V. (1966) 'The Economics of Moral Hazard: Comment', *American Economic Review*, vol. 58, pp. 531–7.

Petri, F. (1978) 'The Difference between Long-Period and Short-Period General Equilibrium and the Capital Theory Controversy', *Australian Economic Papers*, vol. 12, pp. 246–60.

Phelps, E. S. (ed.) (1970) *Micro Foundations of Employment and Inflation Theory*, New York, Norton.

Radner, R. (1970) 'Problems in the Theory of Markets Under Uncertainty', *American Economic Review*, Papers and Proceedings, pp. 454–60.

Rees, A. (1970) 'On Equilibrium in Labour Markets', *Journal of Political Economy*, vol. 78, pp. 306–10.

Ricardo, D. (1817) *On The Principles of Political Economy and Taxation*, vol. I of *The Works of David Ricardo*, ed. P. Sraffa, Cambridge, Cambridge University Press (1951).

Ricardo, D. (Works VIII) *The Works of David Ricardo, Volume VIII, Letters 1819–1821*, ed. P. Sraffa, Cambridge, Cambridge University Press (1952).

Roberts, J. and Sonnenschein, H. (1977) 'On the Foundation of the Theory of Monopolistic Competition', *Econometrica*, vol. 45, pp. 101–13.

Robinson, J. (1953) 'The Production Function and the Theory of Capital', *Review of Economic Studies*, vol. 21, pp. 81–106. Reprinted in Harcourt and Laing (1971), from which references are taken.

Robinson, J. (1956) *The Accumulation of Capital*, London, Macmillan.

Robinson, J. (1960a) *Exercises in Economic Analysis*, London, Macmillan.

Robinson, J. (1960b) *Collected Economic Papers: Volume II*, Oxford, Blackwell.

Robinson, J. (1961) 'Prelude to a Critique of Economic Theory', *Oxford Economic Papers*, vol. 13, pp. 7–14. Reprinted in Hunt and Schwartz (1972), from which references are taken.

Robinson, J. (1962) *Essays in the Theory of Economic Growth*, London, Macmillan.

Robinson, J. (1964) *Economic Philosophy*, Harmondsworth, Penguin.

Robinson, J. (1965) *Collected Economic Papers: Volume III*, Oxford, Blackwell.

Robinson, J. (1971) *Economic Heresies*, London, Macmillan.

Robinson, J. (1973) *Collected Economic Papers: Volume IV*, Oxford, Blackwell.

Robinson, J. (1975) 'The Unimportance of Reswitching', *Quarterly Journal of Economics*, vol. 89, pp. 33–9.

Robinson, J. (1977) 'What are the Questions?', *Journal of Economic Literature*, vol. 15, pp. 1318–39.

Robinson, J. (1978) *Contributions to Modern Economics*, Oxford, Blackwell.

Robinson, J. (1979) 'Garegnani on Effective Demand', *Cambridge Journal of Economics*, vol. 3, pp. 179–80.

Robinson, J. and Eatwell, J. (1973) *An Introduction to Modern Economics*, New York, McGraw-Hill.

Rogin, L. (1956) *The Meaning and Validity of Economic Theory: A Historical Approach*, New York, Harper.

Roncaglia, A. (1977) 'The Sraffian Revolution', in Weintraub (1977).

Roncaglia, A. (1978) *Sraffa and the Theory of Prices*, New York, Wiley.

Rosdolsky, R. (1956) 'Zur neuren Kritik des Marxchen Gesetzes der fallender Profitrate', *Kyklos*, vol. 9, pp. 208–26.

Rothschild, M. (1973) 'Models of Market Organisation with Imperfect Information', *Journal of Political Economy*, vol. 81, pp. 1283–308.

Ryan, A. (1970) *The Philosophy of the Social Sciences*, London, Macmillan.

Samuelson, P. A. (1943) 'Dynamics, Statics and the Stationary State', *Review of Economics and Statistics*, vol. 25, pp. 58–68.

Samuelson, P. A. (1947) *Foundations of Economic Analysis*, Cambridge, Mass., Harvard University Press.

Samuelson, P. A. (1957) 'Wages and Interest: A Modern Dissection of Marxian Economic Models', *American Economic Review*, vol. 47, pp. 884–912.

Samuelson, P. A. (1962) 'Parable and Realism in Capital Theory: The Surrogate Production Function', *Review of Economic Studies*, vol. 29, pp. 193–206. Reprinted in Harcourt and Laing (1971), from which references are taken.

Samuelson, P. A. (1966) 'A Summing Up', *Quarterly Journal of Economics*, vol. 80, pp. 563–83.

Samuelson, P. A. (1967) 'Irving Fisher and the Theory of Capital', in Fellner (1967), pp. 17–37.

Samuelson, P. A. (1970) 'The "Transformation" from Marxian "Values" to Competitive "Prices": A Process of Rejection and Replacement', *Proceedings of the National Academy of Sciences*, vol. 67, pp. 423–5.

Samuelson, P. A. (1971) 'Understanding the Marxian Notion of Exploitation: A Summary of the so-called Transformation Problem between Marxian Values and Competitive Prices', *Journal of Economic Literature*, vol. 9, pp. 399–431.

Samuelson, P. A. (1973) *Economics*, New York, McGraw-Hill.

Scarf, H. (1960) 'Some Examples of Global Instability of Competitive Equilibria', *International Economic Review*, vol. 1, pp. 157–72.

Scherer, F. M. (1971) *Industrial Market Structure and Economic Performance*, Chicago, Rand McNally.

Schumpeter, J. A. (1912) *The Theory of Economic Development*, Cambridge, Mass., Harvard University Press.

Schumpeter, J. A. (1939) *Business Cycles*, New York, McGraw-Hill.

Schumpeter, J. A. (1942) *Capitalism, Socialism and Democracy*, London, Routledge & Kegan Paul.

Schumpeter, J. A. (1951) *Essays of J. A. Schumpeter* (ed. R. V. Clemence), Reading, Mass., Addison-Wesley.

Schumpeter, J. A. (1952) *Ten Great Economists*, London, Allen & Unwin.

Schumpeter, J. A. (1954) *History of Economic Analysis*, London, Allen & Unwin.

Schwartz, J. (1977) *The Subtle Anatomy of Capitalism*, Santa Monica, Calif., Goodyear.

Scruton, R. (1980) *The Meaning of Conservatism*, Harmondsworth, Penguin.

Senior, N. W. (1836) *Outline of the Science of Political Economy*, London, Library of Economics Reprint (1938).

Seton, F. (1957) 'The "Transformation Problem" ', *Review of Economic Studies*, vol. 24, pp. 149–60. Reprinted in Howard and King (1976), from which references are taken.

Shackle, G. L. S. (1967) *The Years of High Theory*, Cambridge, Cambridge University Press.

Shackle, G. L. S. (1972) *Epistemics and Economics*, Cambridge, Cambridge University Press.

Shackle, G. L. S. (1974) *Keynesian Kaleidics*, Edinburgh, Edinburgh University Press.

Shaikh, A. (1977) 'Marx's Theory of Value and the "Transformation Problem" ', in Schwartz (1977), pp. 106–39.

Shove, G. F. (1933) Review of Hicks (1932), *Economic Journal*, vol. 43, pp. 460–72. Reprinted in Hicks (1932, 1963 edn), from which references are taken.

Smith, A. (1776) *The Wealth of Nations*, London, Methuen (ed. E. Cannan 1904).

Solow, R. (1956) 'A Contribution to the Theory of Economic Growth', *Quarterly Journal of Economics*, vol. 70, pp. 65–94.

Solow, R. (1957) 'Technical Change and the Aggregate Production Function', *Review of Economics and Statistics*, vol. 39, pp. 312–20.

Spaventa, L. (1968) 'Realism without Parables in Capital Theory', *Récherches récentes sur la Fonction de Production*, Namur, Belgium, Centre D'Etudes et de Récherches Universitaire de Namur, pp. 15–45.

Sraffa, P. (1960) *Production of Commodities by Means of Commodities: Prelude to a Critique of Economic Theory*, Cambridge, Cambridge University Press.

Steedman, I. (1975) 'Positive Profits with Negative Surplus Value', *Economic Journal*, vol. 85, pp. 114–23.

Steedman, I. (1977) *Marx After Sraffa*, London, New Left Books.

Steedman, I. (1979a) *Trade Amongst Growing Economies*, Cambridge, Cambridge University Press.

Steedman, I. (ed.) (1979b) *Fundamental Issues in Trade Theory*, New York, St. Martin's Press.

Steedman, I. (1980) 'Basics, Non-Basics and Joint Production', in Pasinetti (1980a), pp. 44–50.

Stigler, G. (1941) *Production and Distribution Theories: The Formative Period*, New York, Macmillan.

Stigler, G. (1952) 'The Ricardian Theory of Value and Distribution', *Journal of Political Economy*, vol. 60, pp. 187–207. Reprinted in Stigler (1965), from which references are taken.

Stigler, G. (1957) 'Perfect Competition, Historically Contemplated', *Journal of Political Economy*, vol. 65, pp. 1–17.

Stigler, G. (1958) 'Ricardo and the 93% Labour Theory of Value', *American Economic Review*, vol. 48, pp. 357–67. Reprinted in Stigler (1965), from which references are taken.

Stigler, G. (1965) *Essays in the History of Economics*, Chicago, University of Chicago Press.

Stiglitz, J. E. (1975) 'Information and Economic Analysis', in Parkin and Nobay (1975).

Stonier, A. W. and Hague, D. C. (1972) *Economic Theory*, London, Longman.

Swan, T. W. (1956) 'Economic Growth and Capital Accumulation', *Economic Record*, vol. 32, pp. 334–61.

Sweezy, P. (1942) *The Theory of Capitalist Development: Principles of Marxian Political Economy*, New York, Dobson.

Sweezy, P. (ed.) (1966) *Karl Marx and the Close of His System*, New York, Kelley.

Tang, A. M., Westfield, J. S. and Worley, J. S. (eds) (1976) *Evolution, Welfare and Time: Essays in Honour of Nicholas Georgescu-Roegen*, Lexington, Mass., Lexington Books.

Tobin, J. (1980) *Asset Accumulation and Economic Activity*, Oxford Blackwell.

Townsend, H. (ed.) (1971) *Price Theory*, Harmondsworth, Penguin.

Ulph, A. M. and Ulph, D. T. (1975) 'Transactions Costs in General Equilibrium: A Survey', *Economica*, vol. 42, pp. 355–72.

Velupillai, K. (1975) 'Irving Fisher on "Switches of Techniques": A Historical Note', *Quarterly Journal of Economics*, vol. 89, pp. 679–80.

Walras, L. (1874) *Elements of Pure Economics*, Edition Définitive, 1926 (trans. W. Jaffe, London, Allen & Unwin 1954).

Walsh, V. and Gram, H. (1980) *Classical and Neoclassical Theories of General Equilibrium*, Oxford, Oxford University Press.

Weintraub, S. (ed.) (1977) *Modern Economic Thought*, Oxford, Blackwell.

Weston, J. F. (1954) 'The Profit Concept and Theory: A Restatement', *Journal of Political Economy*, vol. 62, pp. 152–70.

218 *References*

Wicksell, K. (1893) *Value, Capital and Rent* (trans. S. H. Frowein), London, Allen & Unwin (1954).

Wicksell, K. (1900) 'Marginal Productivity as the Basis of Distribution in Economics', in Lindahl (1958), pp. 93—120.

Wicksell, K. (1901) *Lectures on Political Economy: Volume I* (trans. E. Classen, ed. L. Robbins), London, Macmillan (1934).

Wicksell, K. (1911) 'Böhm-Bawerk's Theory of Capital', in Lindahl (1958), pp. 176—85.

Wicksell, K. (1923) 'A Mathematical Analysis of Dr. Akerman's Problem', in Wicksell (1901), pp. 274—99.

Wicksteed, P. (1894) *An Essay on the Co-ordination of the Laws of Distribution*, London, Macmillan.

Wicksteed, P. (1910) *The Common Sense of Political Economy*, ed. L. Robbins, New York, Kelley (1967).

Winternitz, J. (1948) 'Values and Prices: A Solution to the So-Called Transformation Problem', *Economic Journal*, vol. 58, pp. 276—80.

Name Index

Abraham-Frois, E.   70, 205
Ackerman, G.   140
Akerloff, G. A.   177, 205
Alchian, A. A.   127, 205
Althusser, L.   146, 205
Andrews, P. W. S.   127, 205
Armstrong, P.   66, 205
Arrow, K. J.   79, 85, 91, 120, 124–5, 127, 145, 176, 205
Artis, M. I.   205
Aumann, R. J.   127, 206

Beenstock, M.   206
Benassy, J. P.   177, 206
Berrebi, E.   70, 205
Bhaduri, A.   145, 206
Blaug, M.   92, 102, 163, 203, 206
Bliss, C. J.   77, 145, 155, 203, 206
Böhm-Bawerk, E. von   90–102, 108, 136, 145, 189, 206
Bortkiewicz, L. von   15, 32, 36, 206
Bottomore, T.   206
Bradley, I. G.   24–5, 35, 145, 155, 206
Brechling, F.   209
Bronfenbrenner, M.   127, 206
Brown, M.   206
Buiter, W. H.   177, 206
Burmeister, E.   102, 145, 206

Catephores, G.   36, 66, 213
Champernowne, D. E.   110, 206
Chipman, T. S.   81, 91, 206

Clark, J. B.   101, 103–6, 108–10, 125, 207
Clower, R. W.   172, 174, 207
Cobb, C. W.   105, 110, 207
Coddington, A.   176, 192, 203, 207

Davidson, P.   176, 207
Davis, R. M.   127, 207
Debreu, G.   79, 85, 89, 91, 120, 127, 207
Dixit, A.   145, 155, 207
Dmitriev, V.   15, 36, 207
Dobb, M. H.   24–5, 109, 145–6, 176, 204, 207
Dougherty, C. R. S.   92, 146, 207
Douglas, P. H.   105, 110, 207
Dreze, J.   177, 207

Eatwell, J. E.   25, 66, 146, 155, 176, 207, 215
Engels, F.   204, 212
Erlich, A.   66, 207

Feinberg, R. M.   176, 208
Fellner, W.   208
Fisher, I.   90, 92, 102, 145, 208
Flux, A. W.   104, 208
Friedman, M.   127, 166, 168, 176–7, 203, 204, 208

Gaitskell, H. T. N.   101–2, 208
Garegnani, P.   24, 69, 70, 146, 148, 155, 192, 208
Glyn, A.   66, 205

Subject Index